LET THE CHILDREN COME

Let the Children Come

Children in the Church

PATRICIA HUNT

KINGSWAY PUBLICATIONS

EASTBOURNE

Biblical quotations are from the
Revised Standard Version
copyrighted 1946, 1952, ©1971, 1973 by the
Division of Christian Education of the National Council
of the Churches of Christ in the USA
AV = Authorised Version, Crown copyright
GNB = Good News Bible © American Bible Society 1976,
published by the Bible Societies and Collins.

Front cover photo: The Image Bank
Illustrations by Eileen Maddison

British Library Cataloguing in Publication Data

Hunt, P.J., (Patricia Joan),   1921–
    Let the children come.
    1. Children. Christian life
    I. Title
    248.8′2

ISBN 0–86065–556–3

Printed in Great Britain for
KINGSWAY PUBLICATIONS LTD
Lottbridge Drove, Eastbourne, E Sussex BN23 6NT by
Richard Clay Ltd, Bungay, Suffolk.
Typeset by J&L Composition Ltd, Filey, N. Yorkshire.

Contents

Acknowledgements

I should like to thank all those who have helped me in various ways in the production of this book. The Revd Donald and Mrs Margaret Marr read the entire script, and Miss N Henshall and the Revd A Carver read part of the script. Miss M Edwards and the URC Church at Wilmslow lent me their service book. I should also like to thank Mr G Brattle for giving me permission to quote from *Sing to God*; the National Society and Church House Publishers for permission to quote from *Children in the Way*; The British Council of Churches for permission to quote material from *The Child in the Church* (1984 edition); and the Church Missionary Society for permission to use quotations based on an article in their magazine *Yes*.

1

Let the Children Come . . .

'Let the children come to me' (Lk 18:16). These were
Christ's words to the disciples when they were trying to
keep children away from him, doubtless thinking he was
too busy to talk to them. They were wrong — just as we
are wrong if we fail to bring children to know, love and
serve God today. If we want the best for children, we
shall want to help them 'grow in the grace and knowledge of our Lord and Saviour Jesus Christ' (2 Pet 3:18).
This will be a sound guide to lead them on their way
through life, which must surely be our aim for all the
children who come under our care.

When Jesus said, 'Let the children come to me and do
not stop them,' he added, 'because the kingdom of
heaven belongs to such as these' (Mt 19:14 GNB). How
severe then is our disservice to them if we do not do all in
our power to lead them to that kingdom; we are denying
them a priceless heritage.

Look around your congregation today. Is it comprised
predominantly of middle-aged and elderly ladies? Are
there any teenagers? Are there any young children? If
there are hardly any young people present, then there is
something sadly lacking in the family of God in that
place.

You may feel that children are better separated from
adults in church services and that they learn better if they

7

are in groups with others of their own age. This may be so for some of their learning experiences, but we must remember that children do not only learn from the words they hear from a teacher. They learn equally as much, if not more, from being with adults and doing what the grown-ups do. If we separate children entirely from the worshipping church, they will miss out on a vital part of the Christian experience, for they learn best about the nature of faith by seeing it in others. Where families do things together, the children grow up noting — perhaps subconsciously — which are the important things in their parents' eyes. If parents do not set an example of faith, then it will be hard to expect it in the children.

Most children today have little actual Christian teaching in school. They may learn a little about the Christian religion, just as they learn about other world religions, but this is hardly likely to bring them to a real, loving, living faith in God — a faith which will influence their behaviour and indeed their whole lives.

Children these days are seldom taught the Ten Commandments, so that, for instance, 'Thou shalt have no other gods before me' (Ex 20:3 AV) or 'Thou shalt not steal' (Ex 20:15 AV) mean little or nothing to them. If, however, they learn to believe in God, to trust and obey him, then they have a starting-point in deciding the pattern of their behaviour.

Jesus wants them all to come to him, from the smallest child upwards, and if we are to train them in the love and knowledge and fear of God, then we cannot start too soon. 'We' in this context means clergy, teachers, parents, and all who are responsible for the Christian nurture of the child.

The youngest members of God's family

When can the church expect to start helping parents in the religious upbringing of their children? At five years? At three years? No, we should begin far earlier than that. No child is ever too young to come into God's care and into his house, the church. Small babies can be brought in, for the youngest child is as much a vital part of God's family as any adult. A human family without babies and children has something missing, and God's family is no exception. If we wish the church's work with children to get off to a good start, then we must encourage the parents to bring them when they are very young. That is every child's right and heritage. There is no reason why the baby should not be brought into church in his pram. He is likely to have a certain sensitivity to atmosphere, and a church is probably the largest enclosed space he will encounter in his early months, so he needs to get used to it. If the local church is open during the week, parents can bring in the pram occasionally and just walk quietly round. This will also give the parents a chance to have a close-up look at parts of the church which they have not previously examined.

A baby can be brought to church services

A pram with the child in it can be parked in the aisle near his parents. The earliest months of his life are in some ways the easiest time for a diffident parent to do this sort of thing. People are likely to want to be friendly and to look at the baby and admire him. Such people may well include the children's-work leaders, who will have an opportunity to get to know the baby and his family before the child is of an age to start Sunday school — or whatever form the children's work in the church takes. Likewise, the parents will be able to get to know some of the other members of God's family in the locality. When the child is eventually old enough to start formal learning in the church, then some of the church family will already be familiar to him.

Will the baby be too noisy?

Some parents may be apprehensive lest their baby cries and upsets other worshippers. They feel they would rather wait until the child is a little older before they bring him into church. But this need not be a problem. We can suggest that if the baby does make his presence felt, then the pram can be wheeled out of the service for a while. It is easier if young parents sit near the door so that they can take their baby out with the minimum of disturbance to others. No one is likely to object to a baby merely gurgling to himself and giving the odd shake of his rattle. Such sounds tend to get lost in a large building.

Three parts of the child

Each of us, including babies, have three aspects to our make-up: *body*, *mind* and *spirit*. Parents want the best for their children and most take great care over the development of the child's body and mind. They see that his body is clean and well-clothed; they take great care over his food, weighing it carefully and seeing that, as he gets older, he eats up his greens and other things necessary for proper growth.

His mind too is usually the subject of great concern. Caring parents choose the books and toys which they think will stimulate and stretch the child's mind and, so far as choice is possible, they choose which school he shall attend. All this, they hope, will give him the right sort of outlook on life.

But what of his spirit — often the most neglected

10

side of child-raising? The spiritual side is the most important part of his training in many ways. This is the side which will govern the sort of life he lives, what his moral standards will be, and what sort of words and actions he will deem to be right and which sort he will deem to be wrong. This must include belief, for right actions depend on right belief. Thus the proper nurture of the child's spiritual side can make all the difference to his ultimate way of life and his happiness. It is, therefore, important that the child's beliefs are soundly based. As St Paul wrote to his colleague the young Timothy:

> Hold firmly to the true words that I taught you, as the example for you to follow, and remain in the faith and love that are ours in union with Christ Jesus. Through the power of the Holy Spirit, who lives in us, keep the good things that have been entrusted to you (2 Tim 1:13–14 GNB).

This is sound advice for any follower of Christ.

It would be wrong for parents to think that all this side of life can safely be left to the child's school, or even the church, however good these may be. One mother brought her four-year-old child to a Sunday school for the first time one day and said to the leader, 'He's started asking questions about God, so I thought I'd better bring him to you.' Obviously she felt completely inadequate to cope with the spiritual side of the child's upbringing, and yet she should have been the best person to help him – albeit backed up by the church and possibly the school also.

Parents' influence

The church's leaders and Sunday school teachers will doubtless realise that the most important influence on the growth of any child is that of his parents. Although parents may see that the child attends church and Sunday school, that of itself cannot be of greater significance than the attitudes and behaviour of the parents themselves. It has been said that an ounce of parent is worth a pound of priest, and there is much truth in this; it is also salutary to think that while the church may have the child under its influence for perhaps only 1 hour per week, the parents (and the school) influence him for the other 167 hours in the week. An unequal struggle indeed!

This is not to decry the influence of the church — it can be of great significance — but any work which church or Sunday school can do to help a child's spiritual development is much lessened and hindered if there is little support from the parents. Obviously then a large part of the church's work with children must seek the co-operation of the parents.

'Religion is caught rather than taught' is an old saying with a good deal of truth in it. It goes well with another old motto: 'Actions speak louder than words.' Both these sayings are exemplified in the understanding of how much 'religion' children catch from their parents and other adults around them whom they respect. For instance, the way we speak to a child can often make a deeper impression than the actual words we say. Do we really act as though we love our neighbours (in the biblical sense)? If, for example, we speak and act kindly to other people — children as well as adults — then the children are likely to 'catch' from us a deeper thoughtfulness for others, which is one of the ways in which we can obey Christ's command to 'love one another' (Jn 13:34).

Most people in adult life say they cannot remember any of the lessons they heard when they were children in Sunday school; but a good many people can remember the teacher. A wise old minister once said that he owed his choice of a career in the church to an adult whose manner had influenced him greatly. She had been his Sunday school teacher, and was by no means a clever woman. She had left school at the age of fourteen without any qualifications at all and had worked in a factory. The old minister said that he could not remember the words of any of the lessons she had taught him, but what had deeply impressed him was her manner and the sort of person she was. He felt that if the kind, loving manner which she displayed was due to her religion, then he wanted to become part of that way of life too. So began for him, as quite a young boy, his resolve to become ordained. In all probability, that teacher never knew the influence she had exercised, which should be an encouraging thought to all leaders and teachers of children today.

Conversely, a young teenager of the 1980s, who came from a Christian church-going family, suddenly declared that he wasn't going to church any more. When his puzzled parents asked why, he replied, 'I thought you were supposed to love Jesus, but none of those people who go to church look as though they do — they all look so miserable.' What an indictment against the members of that church!

Christianity is a serious business, but it is also a cheery business and Christians ought to be the most joyful people alive, for we have the wonderful news of the gospel of Christ, the power of God, and the indwelling of the Holy Spirit to help us through all the trials and tribulations of life.

Some people say that we should be concerned that children are attracted to God rather than to ourselves. That is so, up to a point, but God works through people, and while we are on earth we are his human agents — his hands and his feet — therefore the manner of our living and of our worship can either attract other people to God or repel them, and this applies to children as well as adults. The impressions the young gain from us can last a lifetime.

All children learn by imitating, often unconsciously. They do the things they see us do; their games are often an imitation of adult behaviour — 'Let's play doctors and nurses/shopkeepers/schools', etc — whereupon they do as they have seen the adults do, sometimes giving us a rude awakening! Likewise, in the case of parents, 'thoughts' can pass from the adult to the child without a word being spoken. A calm and serene mother makes for a calm and serene child; whereas argumentative parents often have quarrelsome children. So the parents' attitudes towards spiritual matters are of vital importance — far more than perhaps they realise.

An important aspect of this influence is for a parent to *bring* a child to church rather than to *send* him. As one little boy remarked one Sunday morning, 'Mummy, when will I be old enough to stay at home and clean the car with daddy?' If families profess to be Christians, then it seems logical that they should go to the Christians' meetings (ie to church), just as they would attend the gatherings of any other organisation to which they belonged. It would seem odd to hear someone say, 'Oh yes, I'm a member of the Women's Institute (or Round Table or whatever) but I don't go to the meetings. I agree with what they're doing though.' It is equally odd to hear people profess to be Christians and yet never join in the worship or any activities of the church.

Sometimes they say they can be a Christian on their own without meeting their fellow-worshippers. But this is not really so. It is difficult to be Christians on our own; we all need the fellowship and stimulation of others.

How hard it is to 'go it alone' is illustrated by the coals on the fire: if a live coal falls out on to the hearth, it soon dies if it is left there on its own, but if it is put back on the fire, it will soon come to life again and play its part in helping the whole fire to glow. Much the same applies to Christians. We all need the support and encouragement of other members of God's family to help keep our faith glowing and alive. In any case, a group of people working together can usually achieve far more than can a single person struggling on alone. In the church, and elsewhere, we need one another.

So Christians join together and go to church, taking the babies and children with them, and thus the members of God's family meet together for worship, work and fellowship. This is what our work with children is all about.

It is significant that the child and his parents go *as a family* — and that includes the father, a very important person. In Bible times it was the father's responsibility to teach his children the Law and the meaning of the Jewish faith. In these days when so many families break up, one of the ways in which we may help to keep together is by worshipping together as a family.

We all need to pray for our families, both our human family and the local church family to which we belong. Teachers and leaders of children's work will wish to pray for each child in their group, remembering each by name. We should pray that our local church will be able to show its love for its members and so do all in its power to nurture families, both within and outside it. With the strength and power of the Holy Spirit behind us, who knows what we may achieve?

2

Young Children at the Ordinary Services of the Church

The church must not only be prepared to welcome babies in prams at the ordinary services, it must also be able to cater for young toddlers who may not yet be old enough to join the formal Sunday school (or whatever facility is provided for children).[1]

When the ASB Baptism service says we *welcome* the child, it does not mean that we welcome him only for a limited period while he is reasonably static and stays put in his pram. Our welcome must include all the children as they grow up.

Sunday is a special day and it is right that we should encourage people to keep it holy, separate and different from the other days of the week. As children grow up, they can be encouraged to look forward to Sundays as days when we do special things together with the family. One of these things should be going to church to meet with the other members of God's family in the area, so that we may worship him together. We must make it known that we (the church) are anxious to welcome all the children, however young, at these family gatherings.

After worship, the highest priority of the day, it is good for us to enjoy relaxation and recreation together. There is nothing wrong with games on Sundays, providing they do not interfere with worship, which must always come first. God meant Sunday (the Sabbath as it was in early biblical times) to be a day of rest and 're-creation'. (The Sabbath was the seventh day of the week, equivalent to our Saturday. The main day of worship was changed to Sunday, the first day of the week, because the most important event in history — Jesus' resurrection — had happened on that day. It was thus decided that Sunday be the Christians' special holy day, so as to commemorate the resurrection. Every Sunday is therefore a 'little Easter'.)

Coping with small children in church

The thought of coping with a toddler in church makes some parents very wary about bringing them at all. 'He's never still,' they say, justifiably, 'and I know he'd never stay quiet for two minutes!'

But this really need not be a problem for any church which is geared up to tackling the situation sympathetically. Many churches organise a crèche for the youngest members of the congregation and it is usually held during the Morning Service in a room or hall adjacent to or within the church building. The crèche should be well-equipped with a variety of toys and other items necessary for the infants' happiness and staffed by caring, competent church members. The parents can then worship happily and peacefully, knowing that their children are being cared for, and that they themselves are within easy reach should any problem arise.

Sometimes parents say that the baby or toddler would never stay on his own without his mother. In these cases, it can be suggested that mother (or father) goes into the crèche with the child and stays for a while in the room but not too near the child. Then, when the child becomes happily occupied, the parent can creep away and the child will probably never even notice!

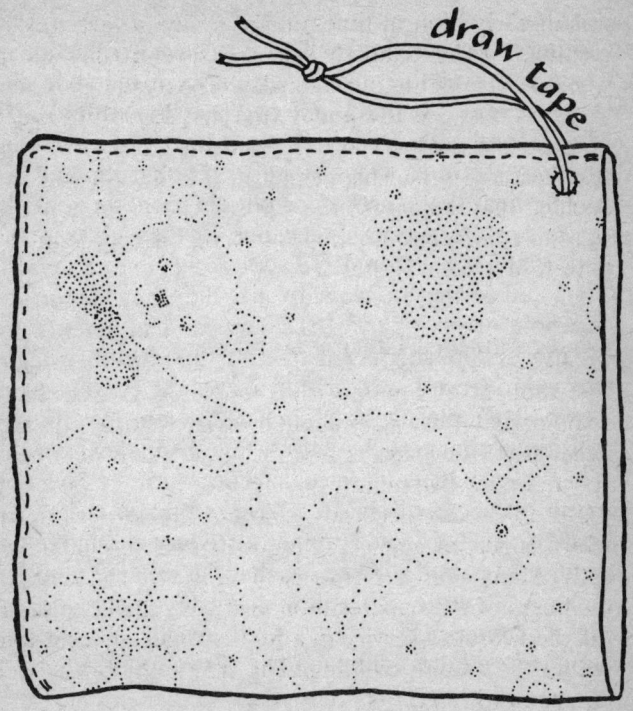

draw tape

a busy bag made of colourful fabric with a drawstring top

'Busy bags'

Another useful idea for toddlers is to have a collection of 'busy bags' available. These are made in the style and size of the old-fashioned shoe bag (see illustration) with a draw-string with which to hang it up. They each contain a few soft toys, crayons, paper, books, etc, and are hung up near the church door on a hatstand or something similar. Parents can take one as they go into the service, and the children are kept occupied and reasonably quiet during the worship, whether they stay in for the whole or only part of the service. The parents are able to worship with less distraction, and the busy bag is returned to its peg as the family leaves the church.

Several people in the church fellowship may be responsible for making the bags, while the majority of the toys — like those used in the crèche — can be given by parents whose own children have outgrown them. An appeal for such toys will probably produce enough to get the busy bags well stocked, so that this scheme, and the crèche, costs little or nothing in money and is a great help to young parents. ('It saved my life last Sunday morning!' said one young mother of two toddlers.)

Pram club

Pram clubs are usually held on a weekday afternoon, perhaps once a month or once a fortnight. Here parents bring their prams, with the baby inside, together with any other pre-school toddlers alongside, to the church hall or place where the pram club meets.

The parents meet together and while this is going on, their children are cared for in another room or at the other end of the hall. Again helpers look after the young, and grannies have been known to be delighted to offer their services for these club afternoons. Teenagers too have proved very helpful — during school or college holidays — although it is advisable to have at least one older adult on hand too.

The pram club has its box of toys, which might be some of the same ones which the other organisations use, and the toddlers come to recognise these 'pram club toys' and often want to play with the favourite ones each time they come.

While the toddlers have the benefit of play with other children in the care of a trusted adult, the mothers can relax over a cup of tea in each other's company; the children may be given orange juice and a biscuit at some suitable point.

Some clubs may organise a programme of talks and discussions about the spiritual upbringing of their children and other related subjects, and these have been found helpful by many parents. On days when there is no organised programme, parents may like to chat and share their ideas and their problems. Whatever happens, no parent need feel isolated, and a group like this is often a help to young mothers who may be tied to the house all day with only the toddler to provide conversation. Often they discover that their own problems are not unique!

If you are looking for speakers and topics for the pram club, have a look round your area and find out what useful people there are available. For instance:

* A children's nurse or nanny may talk about her work with children, perhaps including the problems of deprived children,
* A social worker about his or her work.
* A policeman or safety officer on safety both inside and outside the home.
* A clergyman on the church's attitude to divorce and re-marriage.

* One of the church's children's leaders on the facilities provided for the children as they get older.

Other topics might include:

* Suitable books — both for children and parents.
* How to cope with the death of a child.
* The problems of one-parent families.
* Mentally and physically handicapped children.
* Answering children's difficult questions.
* Beach missions and similar facilities provided for children on holidays.

These are but a few of the many subjects of interest to young parents, who may well suggest other topics themselves.

Some pram clubs also hold a summer picnic, when the parents bring their own food and enjoy a picnic lunch together – a good way to make new friends.

No matter what happens at the pram club, the organisers must allow sufficient time for the parents to be able to meet any older children from school.

The organising of the pram club could be run by a small group of parents and others who agree to serve for one or two years. This would give the opportunity for everyone who wished to have a share in the running of the club, and need not be too onerous on any one person.

Mid-week services

Some churches hold a mid-week service for parents and children who are under school age, when they can come together and learn about God's love and care for them.

This type of service is more relaxed than a normal Sunday service and is one which many parents find easier to cope with while the children are still very young. It gives the clergyman an opportunity to teach in simple terms about the Christian life. The children may be taught short hymns and prayers, and the parents present can learn too and so help the child to use these prayers and hymns at home.

There may be a simple talk for the children, or sometimes one addressed to the parents.

If the clergyman himself takes the service, he can truly be seen as a father-in-God to the little ones, and he may well become someone whom they will recognise and continue to relate to as they grow up in the church family. He will also get to know the young parents better than is possible at a Sunday service. However, there is no reason why these mid-week services should always be taken by the clergyman. The laity can help sometimes and thus give the parents a chance to get to know another member of their church family.

If there is no existing crèche, pram club or mid-week service in the parish, an appeal for anyone interested in such things might well be the starting-point. If parents are willing to help in the running of such things, it could well give them an interest outside the home, and help to overcome any feelings of diffidence which they may have. If they thus become involved with others in the day-to-day work of the church, they will not only get to know their fellow-workers better, but they will also doubtless come to see the church's 'human face' in action.

3
Growing up in the Church

The whole church (ie the people, the body of Christian believers) has a duty to see that children are made welcome in worship, for the duty of Christian welcome is laid on us by none other than Christ himself. In Mt 18:5 he said, 'Whoever receives one such child in my name receives me'; but he also added, 'Whoever causes one of these little ones who believe in me to sin, it would be better for him to have a great millstone fastened round his neck and to be drowned in the depth of the sea' (Mt 18:6). Thus we can see how very much children matter to God.

Part of our duty here is to help the children to feel at home in God's house, which means far more than simply seeing that they are kept quiet and entertained while *we* worship. It really means caring for their whole spiritual lives and helping to nurture them in the faith. Nothing can be more important than this. Children are inheritors of the kingdom of heaven just as we are.

In the United Reformed Church's Infant Baptism Service, the minister specifically asks the congregation to promise to play their part by providing instruction in the gospel, by the example of Christian faith and character, and by the strong support of the family of God in fellowship, prayer and service. This puts the responsibility for the child's spiritual upbringing not only on clergy, teachers, parents and godparents, but on the whole body of believers in the church. Obviously, they cannot all teach or lead children's work, but they can see to it that adequate provision is made for such work and can welcome the child when he comes into God's house.

In many churches today afternoon Sunday school is no longer the norm; instead it is more often held at the same time as the normal Morning Service. There are various ways of operating this system. The children can go into church with their parents as part of their own human family and also as part of the church family, and there they stay for the first fifteen minutes or so of the service. In this way they learn something about worshipping together. Then they go out to their groups held in an adjacent building, nearby hall or some other part of the church. The group-work finishes in time for the parents to collect their children at the end of the service, so that the whole family can all go home together.

Alternatively, some churches begin with the children in their separate groups, and then bring them into church for the last part of the service. This is particularly helpful if the service is Holy Communion, because the children can then go up to the Communion rail with their parents and (if not yet confirmed) receive a blessing. While this is not the whole answer to the presence of children at the Holy Communion Service, it does at least go part of the way. The subject is one which has been under discussion for quite some time.

However, the method used at present made a great impression on one nine-year-old girl. She came joyfully bounding up to her Sunday school leader after the service and said, 'I went up there with all the grown-ups, and the vicar said a special little prayer over me — just for me! It was lovely!' Obviously, the child had felt that she was an important part of God's family, and that she really 'belonged' — as indeed she did. She has since gone on to become a very useful helper with the crèche in the church. It is this sense of belonging which we must all work hard to encourage.

Whether the children go into church at the beginning or the end of the service, the important thing is that they should be there for some of the time. A Sunday school or children's group which operates entirely separately from the main worshipping church is a recipe for disaster, for the children will almost certainly get the impression that what goes on in the church building has nothing at all to do with them.

Leadership

Sunday schools are changing and many use modern methods of teaching to help the children learn about the faith. No longer do children sit in a formal semi-circle around the teacher and read the Bible verse by verse, as was the method in Sunday schools of earlier times. Today they often have drama, visual aids – sometimes including films, film-strips and videos – as well as model-making, drawing, friezes and collages, together with various other activities all designed to help them understand more about God.

In the Anglican Church the dioceses often have training schemes, held perhaps on a deanery basis, for teachers and leaders of work with the church's children. It is rightly felt that no one should be expected to attempt to teach such a vital subject as Christianity without being adequately prepared for it. The days when it was felt that 'anybody' could teach in Sunday school, even a willing but untrained teenager, are happily dying out. Children's souls are far too precious to have anything but the very best nurture that we can provide.

This is not to decry the efforts of volunteer teenagers or anyone else, but rather that they must have some training in order to carry out the task adequately. Certainly we should never put teenagers in charge of the very young, because we think they are the easiest to teach. This is not so, as any inexperienced teacher would soon find out; for these children are at a very impressionable age and first impressions matter a great deal. The leadership must be worthy of the children, otherwise it is unfair to both teacher and taught, so above all we must aim at quality and excellence in our teachers and leaders.

One other point to note when selecting leaders is that such people do not miss out on their worship. 'Helping in Sunday school' is no substitute for worshipping and learning in the church itself. The leaders of the children will need to attend other services of the church so that they do not miss out on worship, the sacraments and the study of God's word. No one can give out what he has not already taken in; the spiritual nourishment of the leaders is of vital importance.

Teenage helpers

What is to be our attitude to teenagers who say they would like to 'teach in the Sunday school'? They must not be turned away out of hand but they must understand that it would be unfair to them, as well as to the children, if they were 'flung in at the deep end' without any training. It must be stressed what an important job it is, and then we may gladly accept their help — but only as helpers to begin with. This means that they will work with an older experienced teacher for at least six to twelve months. They will help by giving out equipment, helping children with their handiwork, finding Bible and other references for older children and even fastening coat buttons and so forth for the youngest. Such help is invaluable to a busy leader, and the teenager will be subconsciously absorbing the 'lesson' as he/she listens to the leader at work.

When the teenager has served a few months and is proving promising, the leader might suggest occasionally that the helper should prepare the activities for the following week or tell the story or do some other part of the session on his/her own. In doing these jobs, the helper gets some practice in the practical side of leading, which will be most useful when he/she is old enough and experienced enough to take full charge of the group.

Generally anyone under sixteen years old is too young to be solely responsible for a class or group, and we must never accept the offers of teenagers to help if their only reason is that they are too old for Sunday school and want to do something which to them seems 'less boring'.

Above all, the serious offer to help should be countered with a suggestion that they join the nearest local training scheme available. The Diocesan Adviser in children's work, or equivalent officer, should be able to give information about this.

Children in the church service

Small children are incapable of sitting still for any length of time and we should not expect them to do so. When they are present at a church service, we will need to hold their attention by helping them to understand something of what is going on. We must, of course, try and keep them as quiet as possible for the sake of other worshippers.

If the church does not have any facilities such as a crèche or 'busy bags' (see page 20), then we may suggest that parents bring something helpful themselves. A special picture-book kept only for church can help a small child realise that the occasion is different from ordinary playtime at home. There are many good Bible story- and picture-books which would be very suitable for this purpose.

Small children sometimes take great delight in kicking the pew in front. It certainly makes a very satisfactory noise from the child's point of view! But it can be alleviated by bringing a pair of old socks to put on over the child's shoes, or bringing his slippers to wear while he is in church.

Apart from these practical considerations, it is important that we all help the children to feel that they are part of the service. If they merely feel that what we are doing has nothing to do with them, then they are hardly likely to feel encouraged to go on coming to church when they are older.

For instance, we can let small children have a hymn-book to hold, just like their parents. It doesn't matter if it is held upside down; if the children stand up and make their own effort at singing with everyone else, they will begin to feel that they are part of what is going on. One young child announced loudly the page number in the prayer-book a second or two before the minister did because he had heard the minister announce it the previous week and had remembered!

If parents bring their own hymnbook or Bible to church, it is a good idea to let the child carry it on the journey, thus showing that he has a part to play.

Sidesmen, incidentally, should beware of giving children the oldest and tattiest books lest they damage the better ones. The sidesmen may think that they are helping the church finances by such actions, but children are apt to notice things like that. Better to risk having the odd book damaged than to make a child feel he isn't really wanted.

There is a part for parents to play in helping children to feel that they really belong. Not only can we suggest to parents that they talk happily to the child about going to church the next Sunday, but they can teach him small parts of the service in readiness for Sundays. Then when the familiar bits come along, the children can join in — with their usual exuberance. These parts may only be 'Amens' or phrases from the Lord's Prayer to begin with, but they will help the child to feel that he is doing his bit and is not there simply on sufferance.

Parents too should try to see that the child is comfortably seated between two adults and, where possible, that there is not another small child immediately in front or behind. There is less likelihood of 'mutual noise' if this is done, but it is not always possible. Obviously one would not move if another family with a small child came to sit nearby.

Punctuality

Another point to note which may make an impression on the child is the manner in which we adults arrive at church. If we arrive late or at the last minute, rushed and breathless, the children will feel that church-going is not of the highest priority, so that you have to be sure to be on time. If we were invited to Buckingham Palace, we would do all in our power to make sure we were not late. Yet sometimes people drift casually into church after the service has started, to worship God who is the King of kings and far greater than any earthly monarch. Children could get the impression that God isn't so very important if we don't do our best to ensure that we are on time to worship him.

At one church a mother stopped en route to talk to a friend; whereupon her small daughter, aged about six, dragged the mother by the sleeve with a cry of 'Come ON, Mummy! We'll miss it!'

If there are genuine circumstances which occasionally prevent one from arriving on time, then it is obviously a case of 'Better late than never.'

'I don't force him to go'

Some parents feel that when a child gets a little older, they should not insist that he goes to church if he doesn't want to; they say that they would not stand in the child's way if he said he wanted to go, but they obviously feel they should not give any active encouragement to help the child make up his mind. How likely are the children to make up their minds in the right way on their own? Unless parents set a good example by their own behaviour, the answer is 'Not very likely.'

Moreover, if the children's friends do not go to church or Sunday school, then the children are more likely to want to stay at home and play in preference to going to church themselves. If parents simply acquiesce with, 'All right, you needn't go if you don't feel like it,' they are really saying that church doesn't matter all that much but that it is nice to go if you haven't anything better to do at the time.

This is the sort of attitude which contributes to the general feeling of apathy which there is towards the church today. It is not that most folk are actively against the church, it is simply that they do not see its vital relevance.

If the children feel that they really 'belong' in the church, that they will have some part to play when they get there, then it is far more likely that they will want to go willingly.

Sometimes parents fear that if they 'insist' on a child going to church, it might put him off for life. Do they likewise fear that the child will be 'put off' dressing himself, eating proper food, or reading and learning because he is firmly encouraged to do such things?

In any case, to expect a child to choose whether he wishes the spiritual side of his life to grow or not is far too great a responsibility to put on young shoulders. We cannot really expect him to know enough to make the right kind of choice at a young age. The fact that he 'doesn't want to' is not really relevant. He probably doesn't want to eat his greens either!

Do we do our best to see that our children read good literature rather than rubbish, or do we let them choose? Obviously, good parents do their best to guide their children, gently but firmly, in such matters.

There are so many flabby standards and immoral attitudes about today which pull children in the wrong directions. They need all the help and guidance they can get to come through this sort of moral mine-field. Children need a firm background on which to lean, so that they may know whether to go in the right (or wrong) direction. Thus they will feel more secure if they know how far and which way to go. If we don't give them a clear lead, then they will feel about as secure as leaning on a jelly!

Naturally, it is not easy, and each child is different and needs different treatment. As children get older, they may rebel for a while, which is part of growing up — a trying out of their wings, as happens in the young of most species. But if they have had the right grounding and training earlier — from their parents and from the church — and if the adults continue to set the right example, then there is every possibility that the young will eventually return to more secure standards, when they have found out for themselves that the lesser ones are wanting.

Excuses

Numerous and varied excuses are put forward by children for absences from church and Sunday school. Apart from the honest 'I wanted to play with my friend', Sunday school leaders hear such reasons as 'Dad wanted me to help in the garden', 'We've moved to a new house and there's a lot to do', 'I've got exams coming and there's a lot of revising', 'We had to go and see Granny', and so on.

Clergy meet similar reasons for people not being at church and no doubt many are quite genuine; but the real problem is where the priorities lie. It seems that worship is very often left to come second (or worse) in the list of things to be done. Can one imagine any of these 'excuses' being offered if there was something like a first-class football match on? 'I can't go to the match because I've got to help to clean the car.'

If a child belonged to, say, a gymnastic class and had to go for extra training at the weekend, wouldn't the parents be likely to put off visiting Granny, asking for the child's help, etc, until *after* the gym class? Why not apply the same principles to the training of the child's spirit?

Adult 'church friends'

Ordinary church members, having welcomed the child at baptism, have their part to play in seeing that he is accepted into God's family as he grows up, and that he feels he *belongs* there. Yet many church people, if asked what they knew about the training of the church's children, would probably refer one to the Sunday school leaders, as though the children were not really the concern of the rest of the church.

In many parishes, a number of the children who come to the Sunday school or Junior Church do not have much parental encouragement or support to do so. The children may come along because their friends do, but their parents may not be connected with the church at all. These cases are almost invariably the ones where the children leave in the early teens or before, simply because they see that their parents have no interest in the church.

This is the point where ordinary people in the church can do a great deal to help. They can become 'in loco parentis' and 'adopt' a child for church purposes. It might be a child, or one or two children, who live near the adult church-goer concerned. The adult can bring the children to church with him and sit with them during the service, thus creating a family feeling. The children are likely to feel better about going to church if they have someone understanding to be with. When this happens, it is wise for the adult 'church friend' to make himself, or herself, known to the child's parents and so allay any possible fears.

Some children seem to be more independent and appear not to need such help, and no adult should force a friendship on a child of this kind. But such are not very many; most children appreciate having a grown-up friend whom they come to trust and with whom they like to talk because they feel that the adult understands.

Such 'church friends' may go on to become informal sponsors, seeing the child through to confirmation, though not, of course, usurping the parents and God-parents in any way. Their role must simply be that of an additional adult friend.

If one of the children who normally comes to church regularly is absent without due cause, then the 'church friend' — or indeed someone else from the congregation

— might visit the home to find out why. In this way the child's family would see that the church really cares about its members, however young, and notices when they are not there. Parents are delighted to discuss their children with anyone who shows a friendly interest, so no such adult need have any fears about visiting.

Some church friends might eventually feel they would like to give more help with the children's work in the church. Perhaps they would not wish to do a full teaching job, but they may be prepared to give a little specific help from time to time, when such things as dramatics, music or handiwork need extra assistance. In this way both children and adults can get to know one another and the church itself becomes more of a family.

'Church friends' can also be invited to join in any of the children's social occasions, where parents may normally come — eg parties, outings, etc — so that the event is given more of a family atmosphere and the children no longer feel part of a separate entity consisting of children and teachers only.

It might also be possible to arrange for adults and children to meet on other occasions which will no doubt become obvious once the possibility is realised.

Another way in which the adults of the church can be of great help to the children is by becoming 'prayer friends'. The adults are each given a list of names of a few children, perhaps all belonging to one of the teaching groups, and they undertake to pray regularly for these children, that the church may be able to bring them to God and that they and their families will grow in grace and in the fear of the Lord. Anyone wishing to become a prayer friend may be invited to come into the children's groups occasionally, merely as an observer. The adults can then put a face to a name and the whole thing becomes more personal.

Becoming a prayer friend is something which even the older, infirm or housebound people in the church fellowship can do. They may not be able to visit the children's groups, but they can be a vital source of prayer support behind the work. There is no reason for people who are less active not to be a most useful part of the work! The children might be encouraged in church to send a card, signed with all their names, to any prayer friend who is housebound; or one or two of the children, in the company of the leader, might visit such a person, who would doubtless be enormously appreciative.

Once again, the use of church friends and prayer friends is of great help to the children in dispelling the notion that Sunday school/Junior Church is not part of the 'real' church and that the children do not belong. Children are more likely to feel apart if their groups have to be held in a building away from the church, so that the children seldom see the inside of the church building, let alone the people who worship there.

A general note on caring

Caring about children — and showing that you care — is an important part of the work of the children's leaders, as well as that of church and prayer friends. To the children and possibly to their parents 'you' (the leader or church friend) represent the church. You may be the only person connected with the church whom they know. To them, you probably *are* the church. (One little girl obviously thought so when she asked her busy leader, 'Do you *live* here?')

So our general behaviour inside and outside the church building will go to form a large part of the child's view of what the church is like. If we behave in a kindly, loving and God-fearing way, the children may well feel that the church is worth further attention. Whereas if we behave unkindly or stupidly, it might well put them off having anything further to do with the church for life. It is a tremendous responsibility and a privilege to be able so to influence a child's spiritual growth.

The Sunday school leader/teacher often has a greater opportunity than the school teacher to show care. Schools usually have larger classes than Sunday schools and also the rigours of a curriculum to which they must keep. Despite all this, many school teachers still find time to be very caring people.

The church, however, usually operates in a more relaxed atmosphere, and usually has more time to give to less able and shy children. Some children do not have much chance to shine in school, because there is often greater competition from their fellows. The church, with its smaller groups can take the opportunity to bring forward such children and give them a chance to feel equal to their peers.

A near-spastic and educationally sub-normal child was once asked if she would like to take the collection in the Sunday school. She positively glowed with pride and pleasure as she did the job! Apparently she had never before been given such a special job to do, probably because people had felt she might find it difficult; from motives of kindness they had simply let her sit quietly. But once she had shown her capabilities, their opinions changed. For several weeks afterwards she arrived early at Sunday school, wanting to know if she could take the collection again. It had to be gently explained to her that other children wanted their turn too, but that she would surely be asked again in the future; so she settled, patiently and happily, to wait. Incidentally she came of a church-going family, and now grown-up, she regularly takes the collection and acts as a sidesman at the evening services.

On the other side of the picture, a rather slow little boy was once put off church and Sunday school for life because a well-meaning and jovial young man teacher had teasingly told the child that he must have 'cloth ears' because he had not understood something. The child was not able to take it as a joke and was deeply offended, with the result that neither he nor his family were seen in that church again.

As well as church friends visiting a child who is absent from church, the leaders/teachers can show great care if they do so as well. Such visits are always appreciated by parents, and if a child is ill, a small gift will show that the young member of God's family is loved — and missed. If it is not possible to visit, the Sunday school can send a picture postcard to a child telling him that he has been missed and that it is hoped he will soon be better. This is some of the best 'outreach' work that the church can undertake.

If a child is in hospital, a gift from the whole of his Sunday group will be appreciated, and it will also teach the rest of the group something about caring. They might each be invited to contribute to, say, a little basket of fruit by bringing an apple, an orange, a banana (provided the leader has checked that the sick child is allowed to have such things). Then if they all sign their names on a 'Get Well' card, the gesture will be much appreciated by the child and his family, and will also have made an impression on the minds of the rest of the group.

Leaders may need to show extra care when a child is being difficult. Why is he acting like this? Maybe he comes from a broken home, is confused and not sure where he really belongs; maybe he has had a raw deal in life and feels the need to draw attention to himself. Such backgrounds may well trigger 'showing off' behaviour, which may really be a cry for help. Once the cause is known, the leader can deal more sensitively with the child.

Sometimes a child may not be well and may be feeling unequal to the effort of keeping up with other children. If this is so, the child can be given a little extra help instead of the leader chiding him for his slowness.

A child in one church regularly forgot to bring her Bible and the Activity Sheet which she had previously taken home to finish off. It was not until the leader talked to the child's mother that it was discovered that the child had a memory problem for which medical treatment was needed; the mother was then able to ensure that the child remembered her Bible each Sunday, and so the problem was solved. Moreover it gave the leader a chance to praise the child for bringing her work and so to be of encouragement to her.

Family Services

Many churches these days hold a Family Service on perhaps one Sunday per month. (The title has caused some comment because it infers that the other services in the church are not for the family, which, of course, they all are. Maybe a better title is needed.)

The idea of these services is that the children stay in church with their parents for the whole service, which is child oriented and basically simple. The address is geared to the children, as are lessons, hymns and prayers. In some churches the children are encouraged to play quite a large part in the running of the service. They act as sidesmen, giving out books and taking the collection, and some of them may form part of the choir. One or two of the older children, carefully chosen, may also read the lessons. They need to be well-rehearsed for this, and to realise the importance of reading God's word in church. They must also be audible, as there is little point in even an articulate child reading a lesson if his voice is not strong enough to be heard in a large building.

If children do take part in a service, it is almost certain that their parents will want to come to see and hear them. In this way even parents who have previously had little or no connection with the church may become interested and want to find out more.

Naturally, even the youngest members of the family of God — the babies and the toddlers — are encouraged to come to the Family Service with their parents. Their chatter will certainly add to the family atmosphere, but if they are too noisy, they can always be taken out for a while. While these services are open to the criticism that they are not liturgical, they do have the merit of attracting 'fringers' some of whom may later be drawn into the wider worshipping life of the church — an excellent result.

Part of the attraction of such services is their simplicity, so that parents who 'missed out' on religion themselves, may understand them better, and probably go on to grow into a deeper faith.

If the very young get used to coming to church with their families, even before they can begin to understand what it is all about, a vital part of their spiritual growth will get off to a good start. It will also help them and their parents to feel at home in the church.

Some people object and say that young children cannot possibly understand what is going on and do not take anything in anyway. The answer to that is that no adult can fully understand God, and that one never knows what a child is taking in. Some of them have surprisingly deep spiritual insight and when we imagine they are comprehending nothing, we are reckoning without the power of the Holy Spirit.

4

Joining in the Activities at Church

In bringing the children into the church family, we are not simply confining them to attending church services. Services are only part of church life in the family of God.

As the child gets older, there are all sorts of church activities other than services in which he can become involved, so that he feels he belongs.

If one of the parents, or some other adult known to the child, is a sidesman, for instance, the child may help him give out the books at one of the ordinary services, apart from 'Family' Services. Children are very enthusiastic helpers on these occasions. At one church the child sidesmen were seen to run out of the church door and thrust a hymnbook into the hands of surprised worshippers before they had even got inside the building. (Could it even be that some who had not intended to come in were given books and lured inside by these compelling little evangelists?!)

On another occasion a small three-year-old watched fascinated as his mother took the collection and went up to the chancel with her plate along with the other sidesmen. When she returned, her son asked in a loud voice, 'What were you doing up there, Mummy?' Mother explained and now when her turn for collection duty comes round her little boy accompanies her all round the building. It obviously makes him feel part of the service, and maybe one day he will do the job on his own.

Giving

While on the subject of the church collection, perhaps one way in which we might help children to feel they are a part of the church is by encouraging them to give even a small proportion of their own money. It is not much use if, when the child asks for collection money, the parents simply give him 5p or 10p of their own. This does nothing to give the child a feeling that he himself has helped, however little he may be contributing. It is much better for the child to feel that he has played his own part.

Two small boys were once on a visit to their aunt in another town. They noticed a missionary box on her desk and asked what it was. The aunt explained, whereupon both boys voluntarily dug into their pockets and put a small coin of their own into the box. The five-year-old then proudly announced, 'Now *we've* helped with that, haven't we?' It was a result which the aunt had neither asked for nor foreseen.

On the subject of giving *to* children, it has been said that we in the comparatively affluent West tend to give our children too much and to spoil them with kindness, but if they are to grow up into kindly, thoughtful people, then children must be encouraged to give. This applies to other things besides money. We should help them to share their toys and their sweets, for instance, and if they offer an adult a sweet, then the adult should accept. It would be a mistake to refuse, on the grounds that one doesn't like taking sweets from children, for this might mean that the child might be discouraged about offering to share anything else. Perhaps we need to emphasise the giving side of life more than we do in our Christian nurture of the children.

Churches have various 'giving' campaigns from time to time, when they ask for things other than money. They may need good used toys or books for instance for children in a poorer area. Children should be invited to give of their own things to help such causes. In one parish, the Salvation Army were asking for toys for destitute children at Christmas. One mother of two suggested that her children sort out any toys in good condition which they no longer wanted, but that they should also give up one toy which they would have preferred to keep for the sake of those less fortunate than themselves. The children did not find this easy, but it was a very good lesson in giving thought for others.

Church events and church jobs

There is no reason why children cannot be included in most of the church's events. The children are as much a part of God's family as adults, and we do not say that adults must be able to do things perfectly before they can use their gifts in God's service. Children are not dissuaded from helping at home and told they cannot help until they are adult! If this were so, they would find many things difficult to experience.

Decorating at festivals

This is one of the regular church jobs in which children may be encouraged to do their bit. We can invite their help when the church is being decorated at Easter, Christmas and Harvest, for instance. The children will be pleased to be included, and may eagerly volunteer once the need is known. They may even feel a little harmless pride when they survey their efforts on the following Sunday! Some adults may feel that the children simply get in the way and that the adults would get on better without them. But we should remember that the children are helping in the work of the church and that this is something much to be encouraged.

One Easter a church was including an Easter garden among its decorations. The children had been asked if they would like to bring any small plants and flowers to put in. A group of the noisiest and most boisterous boys at once volunteered to come and help, and the leader in charge feared for the result. She saw the possible ruination of the carefully planned garden! She need not have feared. One of the boys began sorting carefully through the plants, and pulled out one, saying reverently, 'Hey, Miss! That one's just right for Jesus, isn't it? Forget Me Not.'

The children might be asked to bring their own offerings for other parts of the church too. It does not matter if the flowers consist merely of a few buttercups and daisies in a jamjar. The point is that they are the child's own offering and just as acceptable to God as the expensive flower arrangement done by the flower club.

Children can also help — as they enjoy doing in the kitchen at home — by doing little jobs, such as bringing a vase or some greenery to a hard-pressed adult who may be balancing precariously halfway up a pillar and does not wish to keep climbing down; or by helping to fill a tray with damp sand, or by helping to sweep up the aisles and put the rubbish in a sack or bucket. At harvest time we can encourage the children to bring their own offerings, if possible those which they have had some hand in preparing, eg some vegetables which they have washed or scrubbed clean, some apples which they have polished until they shone, some flowers which they have grown in their own patch of garden. Some children may like to help make up strawberry baskets containing a variety of fruits and/or vegetables and flowers, and these can be taken out to sick or housebound people afterwards. The baskets will be especially welcomed if the child is able to go with the person who delivers it.

Bazaars and sales of work

Children enjoy helping at these events. They can help to set out the stalls, put the bought goods into bags for the customers, hand round the refreshments, and so on. In this way they get to know adults — and the adults get to know them — and they are helping towards the work of the church, and so making their own offering to God. There may also be some games in the running of which the children can do their part.

Delivering literature

Provided there is some adult supervision to see that the job is done properly, there is no reason why older children should not help with delivering the church magazine and other literature round the parish. Even small children would enjoy walking round (or pedalling round) with an adult and being given the magazine to 'post' in the house letter-boxes.

In the churchyard

Churchyards and the precincts of churches have to be kept tidy. If a parent helps with these sorts of jobs — tidying or gardening — a child who may well feel too old to be treated as one of the Sunday school, can thoroughly enjoy the activity as well as being a great help.

The choir and the bells

Children may be encouraged to join the church choir if they have any musical talent. Older children might become interested in bell-ringing, an activity which engenders great enthusiasm. One girl ringer (now adult) traced her lifelong interest in bells back to the days when she had been taken up the bell-tower when the Sunday school were doing a course on the church building; she had been a keen ringer ever since.

Visiting

If a parent goes to visit the sick or elderly, a child might sometimes go too. This may need a little care, as not all sick people would benefit from the presence of a child. The elderly, however, especially those who live on their own, are often immensely cheered by the sight of a young face. It is good for the children too, for there is often a strong bond between the very young and the very old.

When a child is taken on such a visit, it is good if he can take along some small gift of his own. It may only be a card which he has drawn or coloured, but the recipient will invariably be delighted with it.

By encouraging such participation, both inside and outside the church building, we are helping children to see the Christian life in action and that 'outreach' to others is one of its main tasks. We are also demonstrating that there is greater happiness in giving than in receiving.

One Sunday school takes the children to a local old people's home each Christmas to sing carols. The children take with them Christmas cards which they have made themselves; every resident gets a card, and sometimes the staff too, all handed over by the proud designers. Sometimes it may be the only card from outside which the person receives, and in at least one case the card was kept for a whole year by an old lady, who produced it the next Christmas and asked, 'Is the "young man" who brought me this coming again this year?'

Books for underdeveloped countries

When the 'Feed the Minds' campaign (for sending literature to poorer countries) was at its height, the Sunday school in one parish was eager to help. Normally the children were given a Christian book as a present from the church each Christmas; that year they were asked if any of them would like to volunteer to give up their book so that it, or the money which the church would have spent on it, might be sent to someone else in greater need. There was no compulsion — it was merely a tentative suggestion — and the children were told that the church would still be very happy to give them a book as usual if they so wished. Many of the children came from reasonable homes, and it was felt that this scheme would not really deprive the children in many cases.

'You can have mine; I've got some books already,' offered a sturdy youngster from a farm, and several other children offered likewise. In all twenty-eight children volunteered to help the campaign in that way. The Feed the Minds headquarters was so pleased with this response that they sent each child a brochure and a special Feed the Minds badge which, needless to say, the children wore with great pride.

Jumble-sales for charity

On another occasion two boys organised their own jumble-sale for one of their church's charities. Without any adult prompting, they went out each evening after school and collected jumble from their friends and neighbours. Soon the back bedroom of one of the boy's houses was full to overflowing. They then set about booking a small hall nearby, and here their mothers

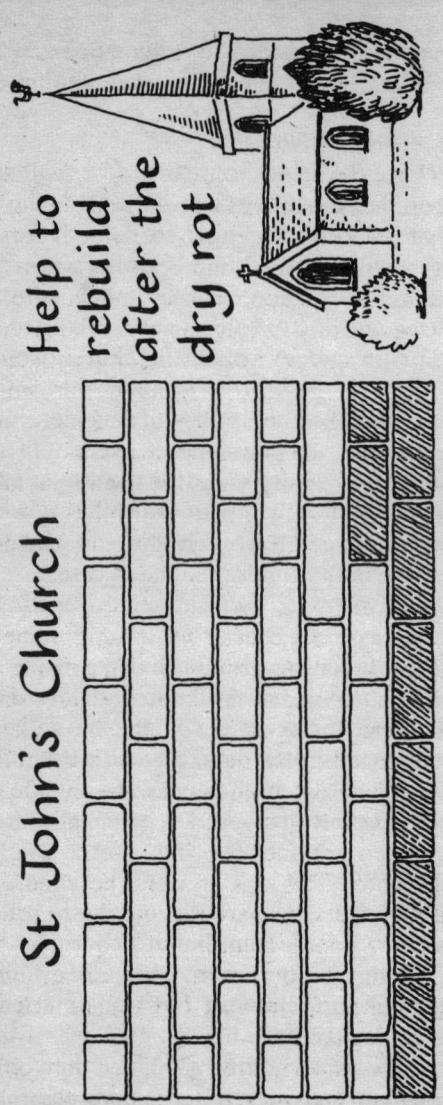

Help to rebuild after the dry rot

St John's Church

stepped in and lent a hand. The result was a very success-
ful jumble-sale and a considerable increase in the charity's
funds.

Helping the dry-rot

When a certain church had an outbreak of dry-rot, it
was felt that the Sunday school should help because the
building was as much *their* building as the adults. So they
started a simple collection chart in the shape of a brick
wall, showing outlined bricks. For every 1p brought (in
addition to the normal Sunday school collection) the
children shaded in one of the bricks in a brown crayon,
and thus the wall grew visibly. When it was completely
coloured, the money was handed over to a very pleased
church treasurer. Here again, the children had taken
part and no one had objected that they were too young
to be involved in the problems of church finance.

A 'home-made' concert

On another occasion a church was raising money for an
orphanage in India. A group of enterprising Sunday
school children decided to do their part and organised a
summer concert in the garage at the house of one of
them. The garage formed the stage, with the roller door
as a curtain. The invited audience (mainly adult) sat in
the drive on a variety of stools, kitchen chairs and boxes,
having paid their entrance fees into a large and hopeful-
looking shoe box. This was entirely the children's own
effort and they felt they were playing their part in helping children in a poorer country.

In return, when a local missionary came home from
India, the children found that India has much to teach
the people of this land.

It is the aim that children shall see not only these
practical jobs and activities, but also the worship of God,

as natural things for a Christian to do. Children learn much by imitation, and so if the parents are seen to be involved happily in work and worship, then the children will follow their examples.

The fact that we often leave children out of church happenings may well be one of the reasons why we lose so many of them at the teenage stage. They simply have not seen that they are part of the church's work and worship, and so they feel there is nothing in it for them.

We should ask the parents to join in wherever possible. As was mentioned earlier, if a child is merely *sent* to church or Sunday school, or to take part in church events while the parents stay at home, put their feet up or wash the car, then the child will naturally think that he can do the same when he gets older. In his eyes, God and the church will be something which you throw off in favour of other things when you grow up.

Getting to know the church building

It has been suggested earlier that a young baby might be walked around the church when it was empty, merely to get used to a large space. Older children can benefit too by being allowed to look around the church when there is no service taking place. At Sunday services, especially if the church is fairly full and the child not very tall, he may not be able to see much apart from the backs of the people in front of him; no wonder he thinks the church a dull sort of place!

If, however, he can be taken in and allowed to look at things closely, then the church and the things that happen in it will have far more meaning for him. We should encourage parents (perhaps in small groups) to bring their children on weekdays.

Let each child have a good look at the **font** — even

inside it — and explain that this is where babies, and sometimes older people, come when they are made members of God's family. It may be that the child himself was baptised at the same font.

The church may have a **baptismal roll** (which lists the names of those baptised there) and the child's own name may be on it, if that is the place where he was baptised. If so, he can find his own name. Few things are more likely to make a child (or an adult) feel that he belongs to and is of importance to any organisation than seeing his name written there.

The child will also like to have a close-up of the **altar or holy table**, and to see where the priest prepares the bread and wine when God's family comes together for Holy Communion. Any carvings, embroideries or decoration may be examined in detail, both on the altar and elsewhere in the church.

The child will also like to have a close-up of the **lectern** or reading-desk, especially if it is an interesting shape such as an eagle; he will also like to see closely the big Bible which it carries.

He will probably like to look at the **pulpit**, which may have interesting carvings on it, and he may even like to stand in it — to see what it feels like to be the preacher. (It could start him off on a new career!)

The **choirstalls** may be looked at as the place where the choir sits. Explain that they are people who are interested in singing and come together each week to practise for the Sunday services, so that the worship of God will be as perfect and beautiful as they can possibly make it.

If the church has any **banners** these can be examined closely, and the organisation which they represent (Scouts, Guides, Mothers' Union, British Legion, etc) can be discussed.

The child can also look at the **windows** of the church, especially if they are of stained glass. He may be interested to know that in very old churches, such windows were put in before most people could read; so that there could be a picture of a Bible story or a saint for them to look at. Stained glass, in both old and newer churches, is also there in order to make the building as beautiful as possible.

Of the **symbols** which a child may ask about, the following are among the most likely to be seen:

> **INRI** (usually found above the head of Christ on a crucifix) — the initial letters of the Latin words for 'Jesus of Nazareth, King of the Jews' (Iesus Nazarenus Rex Iudaeorum). These were the words which the Roman governor, Pontius Pilate, wrote and put on the cross when Jesus was crucified (Jn 19:19).
>
> **IHC** or **IHS** — the first three letters of the Greek word for Jesus (Ihcoyc).
>
> **XP** — the first two letters of the Greek word for Christ (Xpictoc).
>
> **ΑΩ** (Alpha and Omega) — the first and last letters of the Greek alphabet, ie the beginning and the end. They remind us that Jesus is the beginning and the end of all things. He always was and always will be present (Rev 1:8).
>
> **A fish** — Ichthus (from the Greek word for 'fish'). This was originally a secret sign used by the early Christians when they were being persecuted and driven underground. The initial letters of the phrase 'Jesus Christ, Son of God, Saviour' spell the Greek word for 'fish'. So, by drawing a fish, the Christians were declaring their faith.

Significant colours in churches

Some churches use specific colours (liturgical colours) at certain times of the year. They may be seen on the altar hangings, on the pulpit fall (hanging from the desk on the pulpit), as bookmarks, and so on. The main ones used are:

Violet or purple (the colour of penitence) for the seasons of Advent (four weeks before Christmas) and Lent (forty days before Easter, not counting Sundays — ie beginning on Ash Wednesday).

In some churches, **unbleached linen** may be used in Lent and **black** on Good Friday.

White or Gold (festival colours) for Christmas, Easter, Ascension and some Saints' days.

Red (the colour of fire and blood) at Whitsuntide, to remind us of the coming of the Holy Spirit to the disciples like tongues of fire on the first Whitsunday or Pentecost (Acts 2:1–11); and also on festivals of martyrs to remind us of the blood they shed and the sacrifices they made.

Green (the colour of nature) during the seasons of Epiphany and Trinity.

Outside the church

Children may be encouraged to find out whether the church has a **tower**, a **spire**, a **belfry**, a **churchyard cross** (which were sometimes used as outdoor preaching places), a **weather-vane**, a **church porch** (often used as a place of business in medieval times), **gargoyles** (the projecting stone water-spouts at the top of the walls, designed to throw the rainwater from the roof clear of the walls; often these gargoyles are carved in grotesque forms of human faces, animals and birds).

All such close-ups and insights will make the church a more interesting place for the child when he comes on Sundays.

If the church building is locked, as sadly some have to be during the week because of vandalism, then it is worth while obtaining the key for this special purpose.

5

Children's Activities in the Church and in Groups

We have been looking at activities connected with the church which can help to make the children's experience of Christianity meaningful. We also need to consider the activities they undertake when in their own Sunday groups and the part they take in the services, particularly Family Services.

Children remember far more from what they see than from what they only hear; better still, they learn best from things they actually do. So we must see to it that the activities we provide involve their participation.

Small children cannot sit still for very long — nor should they be expected to. The talking needs to be interspersed with actions. In groups they may draw or act each part of the story; in church they may stand to sing, kneel to pray, sit to listen and watch, and sometimes take part in acting, perhaps in the Family Service. The things we ask them to do must be within their capabilities, but not so simple that their minds are not stretched at all.

As a very rough guide, **children up to the age of about six or seven** can be asked, in their groups, to draw; to help make joint friezes or scrap-books; to act; to help to compose a joint prayer; to help in the construction of a model or collage; and to learn things by repetition, which small children usually do very quickly. It has been called the 'golden age of memory', and we should take full advantage of it by teaching great truths while the children are young. Even if they don't fully understand the words, it is better that all children learn something which they can 'grow into' rather than learning something too childishly simple which they eventually 'grow out of'.

On the subject of children's drawings, if you are shown an indecipherable scribble by a proud little artist, never ask, 'What's that?' (You are the leader and you are supposed to know!) Instead say, 'Tell me about your drawing,' and all will be revealed. You may then suggest that they put in so-and-so, which appears to be an important part of the story which the child has forgotten.

Children from ages seven to eleven are able to do everything on the list above, but in a more detailed way. They can also make charts and maps; look up simple Bible references; write prayers, accounts of happenings, imaginary letters and so on; they can also take part in quizzes and puzzles; and learn texts by heart. Learning by heart can often be done as a game; the words can be written up on a blackboard or stuck or Blu-tacked separately to a large sheet; then one word at a time can be removed (not necessarily in order), and each child can be asked to say the text, until they can say it with all the words removed. This can be a team game, with children going 'out' as they make a mistake, and the winning team being the one which survives the longest.

A text can also be taught by using a 'word-search' game. In this, one dash represents each letter of the words, and a vertical stroke denotes the division between the words. The children take it in turns to suggest a letter, which is then filled in wherever it occurs in the text. If it occurs four times, that team gets four marks. Instead of suggesting a letter, a child may make a

G o — | — o | o — | — —

— o — | — | o | o — | — —

g — | — | — | o — | — | — —

God so loved the world that he

gave his only Son... JOHN 3:16

guess at the whole text. If correct, that team has won, but if incorrect, the team loses five marks and the game continues.

These are painless and pleasant ways of learning texts, and children learn better when they are enjoying the activity; so it is well to remember to make the learning fun.

Children over eleven can do more Bible and prayer-book research; they can hold debates; write notes or letters, and compose their own prayers and hymns; they may also do drama.

All ages should be encouraged to do practical things within the church, as suggested on page 43ff.

Generally teachers and leaders should prepare adequately for all activities, making sure there is enough material for every child. It is important to check that the activity proposed will really help the children to understand what is being taught. It is advisable for the leader to try it at home for snags, and to see that what the children are being asked to do is possible for them. Leaders should not accept work which is shoddy when a little further effort would produce a much better result. We should expect the best from the children, and then we are much more likely to get it.

Bible dramatics

Obviously we should do all we can to help the children to love and enjoy the Bible. Acting a Bible story is a useful form of activity, which certainly helps the young to enjoy the story and to remember it. But putting on a full-scale play needs a lot of preparation and rehearsal, even if it is only being performed in front of the other children, and there may not always be sufficient time to do it properly.

The other extreme is simply reading the Bible story

verse by verse. Not only can this be a rather dull way of presenting a story, but it usually results in the children counting up which verse is going to fall to them, putting their finger on it and not listening to the other readers while awaiting their turn. This can be counter-acted, of course, by not having the children reading in order, but by asking them to read at random. Even this method can sometimes seem unexciting and monotonous.

A middle way is to get the children to act simply as they read, using Bibles or by giving them their words on a piece of paper. They can dress up simply, using towels and dressing-gowns and the like, and the leader can act as a narrator: eg 'Then Joseph said . . .' (which should be enough to prod Joseph into action to say his piece). If the children have had a little rehearsal and have under-stood the story, this method can be quite effective. Alternatively, if the children know what the various characters said, they can be left to put the 'speeches' into their own words.

Another method is that of **choral speaking**, which has proved to be an interesting way of reading the Bible dramatically. As many children as possible can be given a part, while those remaining can read together the verses relating to the crowd or other unnamed people in the story. Allotting parts where there is dialogue is fairly easy (especially if one of the newer translations of the Bible is used, where the speeches are set out clearly and are in quotes), but the method can be used for other types of reading.

For instance, in the creation story (Gen 1), several children could take part, each reading what happened on a different day of creation. A whole group could join in such phrases as, 'And there was evening and there was morning, a (third) day' (Gen 1:13). The entire group could join in whenever 'And God saw that it was good' occurred, thus emphasising the words.

In Psalm 150, children could be allotted different instruments to read, and appropriate musical instruments might also be included as an accompaniment.

In the dialogue passages, the children might move about and act certain of the parts as they read them. Much depends on space and the number of children.

In this way, without a lot of prior rehearsal, they will get to know parts of the Bible quite well, and usually will enjoy doing it.

Quizzes

Most children like taking part in quizzes and, despite some modern thinking, seem to enjoy it more if they can take part competitively in teams or groups.

Sunday group quizzes can be devised as a result of a particular session, or they can be general Bible quizzes. (Bible quiz books can be bought.) Older children may write the answers, while all ages can give verbal replies and so score points for their teams.

Sadly, many children do not know the Bible well these days, for it is not so regularly taught outside churches and Sunday schools as was once the case. A quiz may help the children to know more. One method for older children is a Twenty-Questions type of quiz. Each question is written out separately on a card which is then numbered, and the Bible reference where the answer may be found is also given. Each child is then given a sheet of paper with the numbers one to twenty (or however many questions there are in the quiz) written down one side. The question cards may then be placed face downwards on the table, or they may be placed about the room if you have sufficient space, and the children pick them up and answer as many as possible in a given time. Answers should generally be only one or two words. The children will enjoy searching for the answers and, in the process, get to know their way about the Bible better.

A simple Top-of-the-Form type of quiz may also be devised, with two or more teams competing against one another. The questions should be compiled on work which the children have already done and which they ought to be able to answer without too much difficulty.

Compiling a book

This is a different sort of project from the ordinary run of Sunday sessions, and it can be done by the children partly at home, or in weeknight sessions outside Sunday school hours. (Sessions in the week often go down quite well, and often work better if they are for a specific number of weeks, say six, and if there is a group of adults willing to supply orange drinks and biscuits to make a more social occasion. The atmosphere can be more relaxed, and it is an opportunity to get other adults in the church interested in work with children.)

The idea of compiling a book is to get each group to make a scrap-book on some fairly wide subject: eg People Jesus knew; Our church; The church in [some country overseas]; Lives of famous Bible people; Lives of modern followers of Jesus, etc.

The scrap-book may be a large blank exercise book, or it may be home-made by stapling sheets of paper together and covering with a card or large sheet which can be decorated by the children. Inside the children put their own drawings, short written pieces, illustrations cut from magazines and newspapers. The church may have had a visiting speaker on some subject on which the children are making their book — eg a visiting missionary — and there may be an account of the visit in the local paper; this could then be included in the scrap-book. Children may also like to put in their own written prayers and verses of favourite hymns and poems which are relevant. Pictures and maps can also be included, to illustrate the country concerned. If the project is on 'Our church', pictures of the building may be included together with drawings of the various furnishings and short accounts of what parts they play in our worship. This book should also include the people involved, so that the children realise that the church is not just a building, but that it is the people inside it and what they do for God that matter supremely. One such book was beautifully done by some children and was kept at the back of the church, where it formed a useful guide for visitors and attracted much attention.

Younger children can work with older ones, with the older ones doing most of the writing, while the younger ones help with drawing, colouring and cutting out. Working together in this way can stimulate the interest of everybody involved. There is no reason why adults should not help too, for we are never too old to learn something about the kingdom of God.

At the end of the project, the resulting book or books on whatever subject may be displayed in the church for all to see. This will help the older members of the church family to see what the younger ones are doing, and the younger ones will be encouraged by adult interest.

Older children

Sometimes older children say they are 'bored' with Sunday school, and they then fall away (particularly if there is no older group for them to go to such as

Pathfinders, or a youth group, or if they have not been brought up to see the many parts that they can play in the life of the whole church).

There are, however, various ways in which we can help to retain their interest and use their talents in the Sunday groups.

The most obvious (but not suitable for all) is to help with the younger children, but *not* to teach or lead. However, all young people may not wish to become full-time helpers, but may still be of use in the Sunday groups. Full-time teaching help is not always easy to come by and, because of this, some groups of younger children may have to be left on their own at times. Some of the older 'bored-with-Sunday-school' types may be able to help to look after these younger groups in any work they may be doing, such as handiwork, making models, compiling a frieze or collage and so on. Provided the older child has the needs explained, and provided the group teacher or leader starts the work off, then there is no reason why the older child should not be usefully employed in looking after the younger ones as they work.

Other useful jobs they might do are:

Making 'biographies' for use in the junior Sunday school. These are basically simple lives of Bible (or other) characters, eg Moses, Joseph, Elijah, St Paul, Mother Teresa; Bibles are used, where appropriate, together with other reference books, and the biographies are assembled on loose sheets of paper, stapled together with card covers. The young person with the neatest writing should be asked to write the final 'work'. The young people learn quite a lot themselves during this exercise, but it is important to see that they have sufficient reference material to do the job properly.

Making books of prayers. These may be either copied out or home-made prayers or both, and can be used by younger groups in the Sunday school when complete.

Other books, such as a collection of Jesus' parables or his miracles, each written out and illustrated, would be very useful for use with younger groups.

Scrap-books to be sent to hospitals, here and overseas, or for use by handicapped children in this country, have been very well received when made by older Sunday school children, who again feel they are doing something really useful.

A collection of Bible markers can be made on strips of thin card with suitable decorations and coloured ribbons attached. The part of the Bible which they are to mark should be clearly written on the book mark. For instance, 'The story of Moses', the four Gospels — 'Matthew', 'Mark', 'Luke' and 'John' — 'St Paul's first (second and third) missionary journey'. If several copies are made of each bookmark, then a younger class which is working on one of these subjects will save a lot of time each week by having their places already marked.

Embroidery. Girls who are good at this might be able to make or renew lectern Bible markers, pulpit falls, or even banners, for use in the church. Adult help or supervision would be necessary.

Posters. Artistic young people might make posters to advertise church services or forthcoming events.

Charts. They might also make charts which will be needed in future Sunday group sessions. This means looking well ahead at the syllabus and working out what is likely to be needed. It may also be possible for an older child to help to prepare the handiwork for the younger ones for the following week.

Such tasks have the advantage that (a) they are a great help to the teachers/leaders running the Sunday sessions, and (b) they help the older children to feel that they are a part of the working church, and that they are doing their bit to help it along. It helps to give them a feeling of belonging and of responsibility, so that they do not feel that the church has finished with them once they become too old for Sunday school. The object of this work should be clearly explained to the older children, so that they do not feel they are only filling in time with a stop-gap activity.

They can also be given extra jobs to help in the physical running of the Sunday groups too, eg arriving early and ensuring that the chairs, tables, books, handiwork materials and other equipment are ready. They may also find places in Bibles and hymnbooks, marking them (with the markers they have prepared), thus saving time in the group for the main work of teaching the faith. All these somewhat mundane 'chores' are most useful to the group leader.

A library

Books are very expensive these days and many children may not have sight of much Christian literature; one way of encouraging their interest is by setting up a Sunday school library. Once the need is known and a small nucleus of books has been acquired, it may be that parents and others will offer books which their own children have outgrown, and so the library will continue to expand. One should also continue to peruse religious education catalogues and visit Christian bookshops, so that the library may benefit from a few new books per year, thus keeping up to date and not appearing to have only old-fashioned books.

One or more helpers may be recruited as librarians to issue books — perhaps before and after services — and list the names of borrowers with the date borrowed; the librarians also tick off the name when a book is returned, and can remind any child who seems to have had a book for a long time.

The books should be stamped or written inside with the name of the church, and if this is done there is greater hope of having any strays returned. A few books may be lost for ever, by families leaving the town and inadvertently taking a book with them, for instance, but this is not likely to be a great number.

It has been found useful to send a short duplicated note to the parents with the first book which a child takes from the library. The following is a sample of the type of letter which could be sent:

St . . . Junior Church Library

A note to parents: We have started a Junior Library in our church, so that children may have access to more Christian books. To buy such books would probably be too expensive for many children, so we hope you will encourage them to use our library.

When your child brings home a book, as he/she may have done today, may we ask that you encourage the child to read and understand it, and that you try to see that the book is returned within two or three weeks, so that the books have a reasonable chance to circulate?

Should you have any suitable books at home which your children have outgrown, you may care to give them to our library. If you do, we shall be most grateful and you can be sure they will be well used.

While the library is not very large, it may be possible to house it in a plastic toy box which, if put on wheels or casters, can then be wheeled from group to group on Sundays. This has been found very useful when there are books in the library which relate to a particular Sunday session; the leader can show the books and encourage the children to borrow them. As the library grows, however, more permanent accommodation may have to be found. There may be someone in the congregation who will offer to make a bookcase or put up some shelves if asked.

6

Children and Prayer

Prayer is the lifting up of the heart and mind to God; it is talking to him and learning to know him as a friend. We pray because none of us can get on in the Christian life without God (Jn 15:5) and because Jesus taught us to pray (Lk 11:1–13). 'More things are wrought by prayer than this world dreams of', wrote Tennyson with much truth.[2] Things which are often unthinkingly put down to coincidence in this world are often the results of prayer.

It is therefore obvious that clergy and leaders in children's work should back up the parents' efforts to teach children to pray — which means far more than simply teaching them to say 'Amen' to something which they may or may not have listened to.

Just as the first sign of life in a baby is its breathing, so the first sign of spiritual life in a Christian is prayer; if we wish to grow spiritually, no matter how young or old we may be, we must pray — regularly and often. If we only spoke to our family at home once a week or when we wanted something, they would think it a poor sort of relationship. Moreover, if we declared also that we loved our family with all our heart, soul, mind and strength, it would be very doubtful whether anyone would believe us.

Is it not just as unconvincing to claim to be a Christian, a lover of God and a follower of the ways of Christ, and yet not speak to him at least daily? He who is our heavenly Father.

We were made to know, love and serve God, but how can we know him, let alone love him, if there is no regular communication between us? Jesus had a close relationship with God and prayed to him regularly; can we do any less if our aim as Christians is to be like Christ and to train our children in the same way? Those in contact with and leading children in the church have a great responsibility to encourage them in an active prayer life.

As in the case of encouraging parents to bring the child to church, we can never start too early to encourage them to teach the child to pray.

Before the child comes under the influence of the Sunday school, a start can be made by the parents who *pray at the cotside*. Right from the start the child will begin to absorb the fact that this is a natural thing to do. He will be able to sense atmosphere before he can speak or understand, and ultimately he will begin to see something of God through his parents. He will see that prayer is a normal family activity. It is much better — and easier — to introduce him to the spiritual life in this way than to start 'cold' suddenly at three or four years, without his previously having known or absorbed anything of what this side of life is about.

If the child is now beyond the cot stage, parents can still do much to encourage him to pray: by their example, by getting him to join in their prayers and by providing suitable books if he is old enough to use them. Similarly, the church and the children's work leaders can do much to reinforce this training. They can be of maximum help by having a word with the parents to find out how much the child has experienced already. Thus church and family can work together. In teaching children to pray, we are helping them to become friends of God and so giving them a secure foundation in life. We want them to realise that God is someone to whom they can talk at any time in life, no matter where they are.

A small child's religious awareness is caught from those around him, so that the parents' sense of reverence and general sincerity — together with that of the adults he meets in church — will do much to colour his attitude to God. In order to help the child as much as possible both parents and teachers will need to ask God's guidance in their own prayer life.

Using pictures as an aid

Before a child can read, he can learn much through pictures; so it can help in teaching him to pray if there are suitable pictures to hand, both at home and in church. The type of picture needs choosing carefully because the wrong sort of picture could do a lot of harm. Pictures of Jesus should portray him as a strong, loving figure to whom the children will feel attracted — not the weak, effeminate sort of person he is sometimes shown as. Look for pictures of Jesus with a child on his knee or holding his hand, or a picture of him healing someone. 'Here he is with some friends, like you,' we might say, or 'Here he is making someone better.' We can stress how kind he is and how he loves everyone, including all children, 'especially you.' This will bring Jesus right into the present.

We should avoid talking about Jesus in the past tense, as though he were some historical hero, brave and good, who only cared for people long ago. Teachers and parents must help children to see that he is alive today and that he cares for us just as much as he cared for people when he was on earth. 'He is so wonderful that he can be everywhere at once, even though we cannot see him,' we can say. This should inspire a sense of awe.

It is tempting to show small children pictures of the baby Jesus born at Christmas, and while there is nothing basically wrong in this, we do need also to talk of him as a man, especially while we are teaching about prayer. Understandably, children may find the idea of talking to a baby difficult. We can certainly tell them about his coming to earth as a baby, just like us, but we must also say that he grew up to be the most wonderful person who has ever lived.

As children grow older, it will also be wise to veer away from such words as 'meek and mild' when describing Jesus. These words have altered in meaning somewhat, and children (boys particularly) prefer their heroes to be strong and brave, someone to whom they can look up and imitate. Therefore we might show pictures of Jesus standing unafraid before Pilate and his enemies, or riding bravely into Jerusalem on the first Palm Sunday, knowing full well that he was soon to be crucified. That is the sort of picture more likely to appeal to older children — someone whom they would be likely to want to follow.

At first a young child may be content to listen to his parents praying; then he will want to join in himself, and may even remind the parents of something they have left out; eventually he will want to pray on his own. A four-year-old, who did not want to pray with her parents one evening, said, 'I want to say my prayers inside myself today.' And why not?

In church or Sunday groups a child may well put in a loud comment of his own in the prayer, and we should not discourage this. At least it shows that he is listening, when perhaps we think he is not. (As witness a small boy who was keen on aeroplanes, and who heard the vicar pray for 'unity, peace and concord'; he remarked conversationally, 'I've got a Concorde too'!)

If we are using a child's book of prayers which is illustrated, it helps if the children can be shown the picture. This is easier for parents than it is in church, but the Sunday group leaders may be able to show pictures to their group. In any case, even children who can't read will soon learn which words go with which picture, and will 'read' the prayer long before they have any idea of the letters. The pictures then become firmly associated in the children's minds with the words — hence the importance of choosing the right pictures.

If we encourage parents to pray with their children, even as they get beyond the baby stage, the children will begin to see that prayer is not only something which God's family all do when they meet together in God's house on a Sunday, but that it is also something which families do privately in their own homes. It is certain that the child's Sunday worship will gradually become all the more real to him if he has already assimilated something of what prayer is about at home. It will also help to dispel any idea that religion, including prayer, is only for Sundays.

Parents at home can encourage prayer about some of the subjects which have been or will be prayed about in church. For instance, if the Harvest Festival is near, parents may suggest that prayers at home should include a special thank-you to God for some of the food they have enjoyed that day, and children can be warned to look forward to next Sunday when prayers will be said in church (and hymns sung) about God's wonderful gifts to us.

Using simple words

No complicated or set forms of words are needed for prayer (though, of course, they have their place in the church services) because prayer is simply talking to God, and should be as natural as talking to one another.

Long prayers are not necessary with children. Parents can simply suggest that children thank God for a restful night, when they pray in the morning, and that they ask for his help through the coming day. At grace before meals, children can thank him for food, and also remember those who have little. At night they can thank him for good things which have happened during the day, tell him they are sorry for any wrongs done or said, and ask for help to do better. They can also ask his blessing on family or friends.

In the Sunday groups we can pray for similar things, perhaps remembering by name any child in the group who is ill, and thanking God for specific blessings.

Such simple forms can be the basis for prayers with children, and can greatly expand on the limited 'God-bless-Mummy-God-bless-Daddy-and-make-me-a-good-girl-Amen' type of prayer. Apart from its narrow horizons, a prayer such as this, if it is all a child says, completely excludes praise, confession and thanksgiving. It merely treats God as a universal supplier who is only there to be asked for things, and thus builds up an inadequate relationship.

There is a story about a soldier who was in the thick of battle. At one point he got very frightened and said to a fellow-soldier nearby, 'I'm scared; I want to pray. It's all we can do.' 'All right, pray', replied his companion. Whereupon the soldier closed his eyes and fervently prayed, 'God bless Mum, God bless Dad, and make me a good chap. Amen.' While he had obviously been taught something about prayer as a child, he had apparently not progressed in it at all as he grew older.

Praying to someone

It is quite easy to teach a child to 'say his prayers'. It is rather like teaching him to count, say the alphabet, or recite a nursery rhyme. But that is not really praying; it is merely memorising the words of a prayer. Knowing how to pray is a greater and much more wonderful experience than that.

The young child will almost certainly get his first ideas of prayer from his parents. For instance, when they say, 'Now it is prayer time', they should do so with a smile, thus suggesting that it is a happy activity and not some dull routine job which has to be got through. The child will learn almost as much from the parents' attitude as from the words they say.

As he becomes more able in speech, he will need a real person to talk to. We cannot expect him to talk to someone he doesn't know; therefore he will need to know something of God through Jesus. The more he learns of God, the more will he be able to talk to him naturally.

The adults' bearing

The way the adults act towards prayer can be very helpful to a child. If we are quiet and kneel or stand with bowed head, the child will soon copy. We should not worry too much, however, if the child decides to sit down, lie down, or even wander about; if we go on praying, he will come and join in sooner or later, particularly if we look happy about it.

If, however, the child is in a very boisterous mood, it may be useless to try to get him to quieten down for prayer. Instead, we might take the opportunity to thank God for the child's health and strength, his happiness and sense of fun. This is better than giving up completely, and so giving the child the impression that prayer doesn't matter if you don't happen to be feeling like it.

Do not leave out the Holy Spirit

Above all, do not give up because you think the child is not getting anything from prayer. Though a young child is very active and unable to concentrate for very long, we can never tell how much he is taking in. A wise scholar once said, 'Remember that God's Holy Spirit is at work, and you cannot know how he may be influencing the child's mind. If you give up only on what you see as a human, you reckon without the mighty power of God.' This is true too of the child's demeanour in church and in groups, and should encourage all workers with children.

Home-made prayer-books

Both at home and in church children will enjoy making their own prayer-books. These can be made quite simply by stapling a few sheets of blank paper together and putting on coloured sheets or cards for the covers. The children can then cut out pictures from magazines, etc, and paste them in their books as a reminder of people and things to pray about and to thank God for. They can be encouraged to learn and put in their books simple Bible verses, parts of hymns and perhaps the church service, while older children may include their own original prayers.

These books can grow with the child; and if they take them home from church and use them at home, they will become much more personal and valuable than any printed book where everything is already laid out.

There are however several printed books of prayers

for children which are very helpful and which the children can be encouraged to use in addition to their own home-made ones.

Repetition in prayer

Children love to repeat things they have heard — it is an excellent way of learning — and it can be a great aid in helping them to pray, even if they don't fully understand the words to begin with.

While it is important to let the child talk to God in his own language, it is also valuable if he can learn certain great prayers to say — prayers which he will 'grow into' and which will become more valuable as he begins to understand the depth of their meaning.

However, we should avoid the type of prayer which is well-meaning but so worded that it is likely to mean little or nothing to a child. For instance:

> Gentle Jesus, meek and mild,
> Look upon a little child,
> Pity my simplicity,
> Suffer me to come to thee.[3]

The thought may be fine but a child is not likely to make much of it. As was mentioned earlier, the words 'meek and mild' are likely to convey the wrong sort of meaning to a child; 'Pity my simplicity' is usually connected in some vague way by children with mice (by running the second and third words of the third line together), and 'suffer' in a child's mind is usually something to do with being hurt; so that the repetition of this type of prayer is of doubtful value to a young child.

Nevertheless, the saying of some prayers of which they cannot yet fully understand the meaning is by no means always a bad thing. Once they know the words, which may be explained, they can come to appreciate the meaning later. It is good for some prayers to be repeated regularly so that they become known, but we also need to teach our children to vary their prayers so that they fit in with what is happening each day — and every day brings some new revelation to a child. In this way he will begin to understand that prayer is an important activity much connected with everyday life.

The saying of the **Lord's Prayer** is much to be encouraged, even though the child can only gradually come to understand its meaning. At least, it is a universal prayer which he can 'grow into' rather than grow out of. It will stand him in good stead all his life, and as a child's early years are the golden age of memory, full advantage should be taken of it.

The Lord's Prayer is full of meaning, but here is one way in which its phrases might be simply interpreted to a child:

Our Father — God is Father to us all who want to live as his children, however old, young, rich or poor we may be, and whatever our race or colour. The Prayer is an unselfish prayer: we do not begin '*My* Father', we say '*Our* Father'. He is like the very best sort of father you can think of, and much more than that.

Who art in heaven — This reminds us of God's greatness, his majesty, and his glory. He is greater than, and beyond, this world, and much more wonderful than any earthly king — but yet all the time he is very near to us.

Hallowed be thy name — To 'hallow' anything is to honour it, to make it holy. So we are saying that we want God and his name to be kept holy. We can do that by worshipping him in church, by our private prayers, and above all, by the way we live. We never use God's name (or that of Jesus) as a swear word; it is far too special for that. It used to be common to bow one's head whenever the name of Jesus was spoken; this was not an outward show, it was merely a reminder of how special Jesus is.

Thy kingdom come — This means, 'May God's kingdom grow until everybody follows his way,' and the world would then be a wonderful place. God's kingdom (his way, which is always the best) can begin to grow in us right now, if we start living in the way he wants us to live.

Thy will be done on earth as it is in heaven — God's will will be done on earth when everyone obeys him and follows his laws. The world cannot be happy until it follows the Maker's instructions. This is God's world and he made it, and it follows that things will only go right when they go his way. (Just as any mechanical toy, for instance, will only work properly if we follow the instructions of the maker.)

(*Note*: We are now halfway through the Lord's Prayer and still we have not asked for anything for ourselves. It is a pattern for all prayers.)

Give us this day our daily bread — Now we begin the asking part. 'Bread' covers food for our bodies, our minds and our souls, so that we may be fit to follow Jesus. We also think of the millions of people in the world who do not have enough to eat and who have not yet heard the good news of God. If we could remember to share all the things we enjoy, then more people might well have each day their daily bread. This includes sharing our money. Much of the suffering in the world is caused by people being selfish and greedy.

And forgive us our trespasses, as we forgive those who trespass against us — To trespass is to sin. If we are truly sorry for any wrong we have done or said or thought, then God will always forgive us and give us a clean start;

but we must also forgive others who have done wrong to us. We ask God to forgive us *as* we forgive others. Being truly sorry for any wrong includes doing all one can to put the matter right.

Lead us not into temptation, but deliver us from evil — Temptation means trial or testing. It is not wrong to be tempted; the wrong comes when we give in to the temptation to do something which we know is not right. When we ask God to deliver us from evil, we are asking him to defend us from all dangers, and that when we are tempted to do wrong, he will give us the strength to do right.

For thine is the kingdom, the power and the glory, for ever and ever – The Lord's Prayer ends as it began: it turns our thoughts to the greatness of God rather than to ourselves. We are saying that all power and all glory belong to God, and that it will never end because God will be there 'for ever and ever'.

Amen — This means 'Truly', 'So be it', 'I agree to that'.

Obviously a small child cannot hope to cope with all these great thoughts; but the interpretation above is suggested for teachers and for parents who might like to take one or two, or several of the thoughts, and help the child to take in something of the meaning. Much will depend on the age of the child.

Some points about prayer and worship

When helping children to learn about worship, whether in church or at home, there are certain points to remember which may help:

1 Quietness

We cannot hope to get much about prayer over to a child if he is noisy or if the atmosphere around him is noisy.

This is not usually so much of a problem in church, where small children can be taken out if too noisy, but at home it can present different sorts of difficulties. The first need is to avoid other household noises and to go somewhere quiet if possible — eg the bedroom — and close the door. It is appreciated that it is not so easy to get away from noise in a small house, but parents should try to ensure that there are no audible noises from radios and TVs. It may be a question of finding a different, quieter time for prayer. It does not have to be in the evening when all the rest of the family is at home; it could be in the middle of the day when mother and small child may be alone at home. Leaders of Sunday groups must also ensure quietness before they begin to pray. Even a small child may come to realise, from the quietness, that there is something special, something different about prayer.

It may not be easy to achieve quietness at first, but it is worth persevering to achieve a satisfactory result. Talk quietly yourself, and do not attempt to start prayers until there is a reasonable degree of co-operation from the children.

When children are taken to church, and they are beginning to realise that other people are there too, we might point out that if the child makes a noise, it makes it harder for other people to pray.

2 Eyes

The traditional way of prayer is for the eyes to be closed. This is not simply a fad — there is a sound reason for it for both children and adults. If your eyes are open and you are looking around you, then your brain is almost certainly thinking, wholly or partly, about the things which it is seeing; therefore it becomes difficult to concentrate one's thoughts on God. Most people find it helpful to keep their eyes closed when talking to God.

However, there are times when it does help in prayer to keep the eyes open — for instance, if you have some particular visual aid at which to look. Maybe it is a picture of Jesus, or a picture of someone for whom you wish to pray or give thanks to God. A young child may be greatly helped if he can see a picture of the person to whom he is praying. Sometimes a cross will help an adult to remember the great sacrifice Jesus made for us. It may also be a book of prayers which you are using. A very beautiful scene — a garden, lovely trees, a landscape — can also inspire a really worshipful feeling. The psalmist said, 'I lift up my eyes to the hills. From whence does my help come? My help comes from the Lord, who made heaven and earth' (Ps 121:1–2). Surely that evokes a most prayerful atmosphere of worship to the great God who has made the whole world.

So, whether the eyes are closed or open in prayer will depend on the circumstances.

3 Hands

For similar reasons we traditionally put our hands together when we say our prayers. If our hands are touching the things around us, then the brain will automatically to some extent be thinking of the objects being touched, whether it be the books in front of you in church, or the things around at home. So clasped hands tend to help concentration in prayer.

4 Sincerity

Children are very good at seeing through us. They know full well when we mean what we say and when we are only putting on an act. So if we only pretend we are praying, whether at home or in church, it won't be long

84

before they realise it. One of the most powerful examples a child can have is that of the truly sincere actions of those around him.

If, at prayer time at home, we are just there to hear the child say his prayers, and are not sincerely taking part in the prayers ourselves, the child is not likely to see prayer as a very meaningful activity.

If you pray with a child with your eyes closed, try to keep them so and not be for ever peeping to see what the child is doing. Admittedly, if a toddler gets up and wanders off in the middle of the prayers at home or in church, a parent will naturally need to look to ensure that he isn't in any danger; but provided he is safe, or safely with an adult, then there should be no need for the adults to keep opening their eyes.

Types of prayer

All prayer and worship is helped by a system, so that we do not pray for or about the same things every day.

There are several different sorts of prayer, and we do well if we can help our children eventually to include them all. We do not want to limit them only to the asking sort of prayer, which tends to use God as a sort of eternal supplier, nor do we wish children to say only 'thank-you' prayers — though those are probably better than the merely asking variety.

A good system, which includes all types of prayer, is easy to remember because the initial letters of the various types of prayer spell the word ACTS when read downwards:

> Adoration — Praising God for the great and wonderful being he is. There are lots of verses in hymns and psalms which praise God and which a child might well be encouraged to use.

Confession — Telling God we are sorry for our sins, and asking him to forgive us and give us the strength not to do the same thing again. In his mercy, he will always forgive us if we are truly sorry.

Thanksgiving — Thanking God for all his wonderful gifts to us, from the big things like sunsets, hills, and snow, to the smaller things like a home, family, clothes, and simple joys like ice-cream. It may help to suggest to children that they think of two things for which to thank God each day.

Supplication — ie Asking prayers:

(a) Asking for other people, which is where the 'God-bless-Mummy' type of prayer fits in, and

(b) Asking for ourselves (put last, appropriately). This includes asking God to be with us and to help us at home, at school and at play.

Examples

Adoration (praising)

This type of prayer might simply be a verse of a hymn, such as

> All things bright and beautiful,
> All creatures great and small,
> All things wise and wonderful,
> The Lord God made them all.[4]

or perhaps for older children,

> O Lord of heaven and earth and sea,
> To thee all praise and glory be!
> How shall we show our love to thee
> Who givest all?[5]

or,

> Let us praise, as we raise heart and voice to God above,
> Let it ring, as we sing out the story of his love.

86

Let it flow, let it grow, let it rise from every shore:
Be adored, Christ the Lord, praise his name for evermore![6]

Confession

Try to encourage a child to make this a real confession
and if, as he gets a little older, he prefers, when praying
with parents at home, to do this silently, then he should
certainly be allowed to do so. A form of confession
might be:

> O Lord Jesus, I am sorry for the wrong and naughty things
> I did today . . ., and for the unkind words I said to . . ., and
> thought about . . . Please forgive me and help me to do
> better tomorrow.

We should also help a child to see that an important
part of being sorry is to apologise to the person wronged,
and to do all that is possible to put things right. This is
the only way he can ever feel happy about it. Moreover,
it should be done as quickly as possible, otherwise it will
become meaningless to the child. 'Do not let the sun go
down on your anger,' wisely advises St Paul (Eph 4:26);
in other words, 'get things put right the same day'.

Thanksgiving

Here we can begin to widen the child's horizons in grati-
tude as he progresses in prayer. He may begin by simply
looking around him and thanking God for his home and
family, his friends, toys, pets, something new, something
exciting. He can then go further and thank God for
church, for good people and kindness shown to him
outside: at school, for the 'lollipop' lady, the policeman,
doctor, nurse, shopkeepers, neighbours; all of which will
help him to realise that everything that is good comes
from God.

Other things which interest a child and for which he might be encouraged to give thanks to God are, for example, animals, zoos, playgrounds (health and strength), roundabouts, parks, games and fun, sunshine, sea, sand, snow, ice, flowers, trees, mountains, and so on. It is not to be expected that any child should recite these things regularly as a list; it is better if one or two of them could be linked to something which has happened that day, so giving the child direct cause to be thankful. Such gifts from God are absolutely numberless and can be varied each day. In Sunday groups children could be asked to suggest ideas.

A rather older child might include a prayer such as: 'Lord Jesus, thank you for dying for me on the cross and for being my Saviour and Friend. May I never let you down in the things I say and do.'

An elderly man, whose life seemed to contain more than an average amount of troubles, remained looking surprisingly happy and cheerful. When asked what was the secret of his apparent happiness, he replied:

> I never go to bed without thanking God for at least two wonderful or beautiful things which I have seen or which have happened to me that day. Most days there are many more than two, and it makes one much more cheerful to think of all the beauty and goodness that there is about. It is just a question of getting into the habit of looking for it.

Supplication

(a) *Asking for others*. This 'God bless . .' type of prayer can be expanded into asking God to bless and help different people in different ways. For example, one can begin with one's family and friends, and go on to those who are sick and in pain, those in trouble or danger, the needy, the hungry and poor, the sad and lonely, the blind, the deaf and the crippled, and those who have not yet heard about Jesus. Even small children, when asked, will be able to suggest people in some of these categories.

If personal names can be put to some of the prayers, then the child's prayer will become more realistic to him: eg 'God, please bless Mrs Jones down the road, who is in a wheel-chair and can't walk; show me if there is anything I can do to cheer her up or to help her.' Or, 'Heavenly Father, bless all people who are ill in hospital, especially John; thank you for the doctors and nurses who are looking after him; show me what I can do to make him feel happier.' (If an idea subsequently comes into the child's head of something which he, and perhaps the others in his group, can take to John, then surely God has answered the prayer, in the way which the child asked.)

(b) *Asking for oneself.* An example of this type of prayer might be,

> Lord Jesus, I want to be like you. Come and live in my heart and make me kind and thoughtful. Help me to work hard and do my best at school and to play games fairly. May I never be selfish and leave others out of my fun.

Group leaders can encourage this type of prayer to be composed on Sundays for use during the week at home. A whole group may jointly compose such prayers. The children will have plenty of suggestions if once encouraged to start; they should be warned, however, not to ask God to do things which they can well do for themselves. It should be pointed out that God has given us brains and hands, and he expects us to use them.

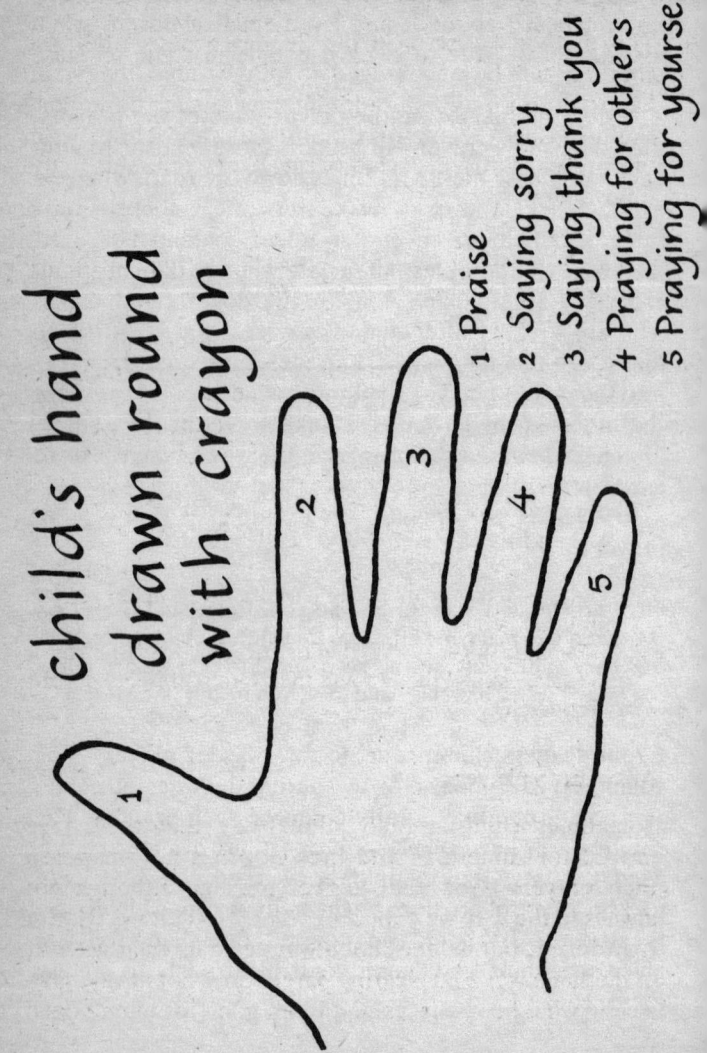

child's hand
drawn round
with crayon

1 Praise
2 Saying sorry
3 Saying thank you
4 Praying for others
5 Praying for yourself

Using the hand to remember the different types of prayer

This method is useful in the Sunday groups when the children can be encouraged to draw round their own hands, with the thumb pointing upwards as in the illustration. They can number the fingers, and either write one or two words on each or write a key at the side in the following way:

1 **The thumb** — PRAISE. The thumb points upwards, to God, and this should remind us of our praises which come first in our prayers.

2 **First finger** — CONFESSION. The pointing finger, pointing to ourselves, and reminding us of the things for which we must say sorry to God.

3 **The middle finger** – THANKSGIVING. This is the tallest finger, and stands for thanksgiving, which should be the biggest part of prayer because there are so many things for which we have to thank God.

4 **The third finger** — ASKING FOR OTHERS. This is the one which wears the wedding ring and so represents love. Thus it stands for the loving part of prayer, ie our prayers for other people.

5 **The little finger** — ASKING FOR YOURSELF. This is the smallest and the last and therefore represents prayers for oneself.

Answers to prayers

Sometimes children (and adults) say that they have prayed for something and that God has not answered their prayers. God *does* answer prayers, although not always in the way we expect or want. God knows what is right for us, but he does not always give us what we ask, in the same way that a caring parent does not always give a child what he wants when it is not good for him to have it.

There are *three* (rather than two) answers to prayer, and we might be reminded of them every time we look at a set of traffic lights: Sometimes God says 'NO' (like the red traffic light), because he knows that what we are asking for is not the best thing for us to have — whatever we may think. Sometimes God says 'WAIT' or 'NOT YET' (like the amber traffic light), because in his wisdom he knows that the time is not yet right for our prayer to be granted. Sometimes God says 'YES' (like the green traffic light), and answers our prayers in the way we ask.

The important thing is to trust God to know what is right, and to go on praying in that knowledge. We must help our children to understand that he is wiser than any of us, and can see much further ahead than we can. If he does not give us what we want, then he has a good reason for not doing so. If his answer seems hard to us, then maybe that is a way of strengthening our characters.

'Everything which happens to us makes for either happiness or character' said a clergyman to his confirmation class, and it is helpful to remember this in connection with supposedly unanswered prayer.

The only way for children (and ourselves) to learn to pray is by actually praying. The art of prayer can only be learnt gradually, and we all — children and adults alike — need to grow in it. Sometimes children's insights can be very helpful to adults, so that learning about prayer is not always a one-sided business with the child learning from the leader or parent.

Like any other worthwhile art, prayer needs practice and perseverance, and adults will need God's help in their own prayer life, so that they will be better able to help the children to be receptive and to learn from them too. We must never reckon without the tremendous enabling power of the Holy Spirit who is helping us all whenever we approach God in prayer.

Sound in worship

The things children hear in church and groups do not only consist of prayers. Worship includes music and readings as well as prayers, and because we have the great responsibility of leading children to worship, we must see to it that all they hear is the very best that we can provide.

Music and hymns

As with prayers, so with hymns, the words should be those which the children will grow into, rather than those which they will eventually grow out of and cast off as babyish. An adult hymn may not yet be fully understood by the children but they can still enjoy it and be learning something which will stand them in good stead as they grow up. Even if there are the occasional big words (like 'Immortal, invisible . .' etc) children often love the sound of them and savour repeating them, and will come to appreciate their meaning later on in life.

There are, of course, some simple children's hymns which are full of meaning and are well worth learning, and these have a place in children's worship, as long as they are basically teaching some aspect of God's truth. If the music set to the hymn is too difficult for children to sing — as some hymn tunes are — then it should be possible to find another tune which will fit the words.

Readings and prayers

Both readings and prayers in church and in Sunday group sessions should be done by someone with a good, clear voice, be it adult or older child. It is often helpful to include prayers which the children have written themselves. If this is done, it is better not to name the author at the beginning of the prayer, because this will result in the other children turning to look at the author or at least thinking about him/her more than the words of the prayer. If the leader names the author at the end of the worship, then this may inspire other children to contribute their own prayers too. This writing of one's own prayers is something much to be encouraged as it is one of the things which helps the children to see that they have a part to play in worship.

If children volunteer to read their own prayers at a group worship session, we must see that their voices are loud enough to be heard by all.

There are many good books of prayers available for use with children, and these may be used to help children compile their own books of prayers as well as for joint worship.

7
Children and the Bible

It is obvious that the Bible is a basic tool for Christian nurture. God speaks through his word. The Bible teaches us not only the facts of our faith, but also gives us the experiences of believers who have gone before us. These experiences are a great inspiration, and must needs be looked at in the light of our own experiences and those of the children whom we are leading to God.

It is important, therefore, particularly with young children, that we use the Bible selectively; some parts of it will 'speak to the children' more readily than others. So we should aim at choosing those parts of the Bible which will have a meaning to children from their own experiences.

The British Council of Churches report *The Child in the Church* (1984) has some interesting paragraphs on this point:

> 80 As an illustration, we may briefly consider the parables of Jesus. In the parables Jesus attempts to convey truth by using metaphors or pictures which his audience understood and with which they were thoroughly familiar. They knew without being told the method by which the Palestinian peasant sowed his seed, and the reason for it. To them these images had a compelling logic of their own. The modern reader of a parable is often in the position of a man who has to have a joke explained to him. The image

which was meant to clarify has become for him something to be clarified. To remain true to the Bible and its method the nurturer ought often to abandon the Bible's own image or story and find an alternative which is *immediately* understood and which makes its own point without the necessity of explanation. It goes without saying that this puts a heavy responsibility on the nurturer to make sure that he, at least, thoroughly understands the original and what it means.

81 The gospel which we present to our children must not be a different gospel from that which we deem appropriate to adults. Neither must our exegesis of the Bible be a different one. Though we must adapt our expression of it to the experience and understanding of the child, the content of what is expressed must remain the same.

82 If we continue to present the Bible to children, we ought to examine carefully our motives for doing so. Bible teaching is often given, not because it really helps the child's understanding, but because it makes the teacher feel better. The teacher tells a Bible story, and tells it well, and feels a great sense of satisfaction, a conviction that something must have been achieved. This is to assume that Bible teaching is somehow self-justifying, an end in itself. But the aim of presenting biblical material is to increase Christian understanding. Where understanding can be more readily promoted by other means, we must cheerfully adopt them.

83 This is not to overlook the educational value of the story, as such. Stories relating to the child's own experience can be very valuable. But the story is not to be used as a *substitute* for the child's own experience, and this is how Bible stories frequently are used.

Choosing parts of the Bible to read in church at Family Services when children are present is not easy. Hardly any Bible passages will mean much to a child unless there is some sort of explanation prior to the reading. This applies to some adults too whom one can see almost automatically 'switching off' when the reader goes to the lectern. It can help if the story or theme is explained as shortly as possible before the lesson is read. In some cases it may be acted by a group of children and/or adults.

If something like this is not done, the children will probably think the reading 'boring' (because it contains words they do not understand) and therefore it will not be likely to inspire them to want to read more.

Bibles by the chairs can be of much help to older children who read fairly fluently and also to adults. Better still, encourage both children and adults to bring their own Bibles to church, providing they bring the version which is being read in church. Adults would not find it a problem if they had a different version — indeed they could find the comparison of interest — but children would soon lose the place if the words read were not exactly those which they were following.

It has been argued that the Bible is not a children's book and that it can lead the child to misconceptions about the Christian faith which will block the road to adult faith in later life. On the other hand, the Bible is so full of great riches that many Christian educators consider it is wrong to deny it to the child and that, provided we are careful in our choice of passages, it is essential to see that the child is instructed in the great truths which the Bible contains.

Even very young children love the simpler Bible stories, such as the Birth of Jesus (Lk 2:1–20) and the Lost Sheep (Lk 15:3–7), and it would not be right to deny them these stories which form a basis for their Christian and moral teaching while they are yet of tender years. If taught sensitively, the children's memories will retain them for ever.

The Bible

The Bible itself is made up of sixty-six separate books. It is divided into two parts, the Old Testament containing thirty-nine books and the New Testament containing twenty-seven books.

The Bible is not simply 'another book'. It is much more important and very different from other books in that it is the word of God, through which God speaks to us. It is true and complete and belief in it is able to change people's lives. We must aim, therefore, to help our children to read and believe it and to understand and obey it; this will lead them towards trusting God and so living their lives for him. The Bible tells the story of man's salvation, which means his delivery from sin and the old way of life into a new life in Christ through the action of God.

The Old Testament tells of the world before Jesus came into it to be its Saviour. It begins with the creation (Gen 1:1–2:4), telling how God made a perfect world and ended by making man in his own likeness. It goes on to explain how sin came into the world through the disobedience of Adam and Eve (Gen 3). We then read how God set about saving the world (salvation) and his dealings with Noah (Gen 6–9) and Abraham (Gen 11–25); the story of the slavery and rescue of the Israelites from Egypt through Moses (Ex 1–15) to the giving of the Ten Commandments (Ex 20). We also read of God's dealings with the kings and prophets, including the stories of Joseph (Gen 37, 39–50), Samuel (1 Sam 3), David (1 Sam 16–2 Sam 24), Daniel (Book of Daniel) and Jonah (Book of Jonah).

The books of poetry and prophecy, such as Ezra, Nehemiah, Job, Psalms, Proverbs, Ecclesiastes, Song of Solomon, Isaiah, Jeremiah, Lamentations, Ezekiel,

Hosea, Joel, Amos, Obadiah, Micah, Nahum, Habakkuk, Zephaniah, Haggai, Zechariah, and Malachi, are mostly too advanced for children and are best left until they are older.

When God told the Israelites that he would be their God and that they would be his people (Gen 17:7–8), this became known as the covenant (an important word in the Bible). When we get to the New Testament, we learn that Jesus himself represents the New Covenant, and through this we are linked through Christ to God.

The New Testament tells of the birth, life, death and resurrection of Jesus Christ and how he came to save the world and to show us what God is like. His life shows us the way of holiness and forgiveness, especially through his death and resurrection.

Following the accounts of the life of Jesus in the four Gospels (Sts Matthew, Mark, Luke and John), we read in the Acts of the Apostles about the life of the early church after Jesus had ascended into heaven and sent the Holy Spirit to strengthen the disciples to continue his work. St Peter and St Paul figure largely here. Jesus' death on the cross and his resurrection thereafter form the heart of the Christian faith. They are like the hub of a wheel, without which the whole structure would fall apart.

The New Testament also includes twenty-one letters or epistles (from Romans to Jude), which were written by St Paul and others for the practical instruction of the young churches which were starting up in various parts of the then known world. These letters, together with the last book of the New Testament, Revelation, are not generally simple enough for children to understand, and it is usually better in Sunday groups to give the children a thorough understanding of the four Gospels and the Acts of the Apostles. The epistles do, however, show the church as the body of believers who want to be saved and who are prepared for a life of service and witness to the world.

We should let the children know that the Bible is a very precious and holy book which should always be treated with care and respect. Have a copy with you when telling a Bible story, even with a class of very young children; you can say that the story they are hearing is 'here, in the Bible', so that at least they will get some idea of its contents even before they are able to read.

Bible story books

There are numerous good Bible story books for children, ranging from 'pop-up' and very-first-reader types to fuller and more detailed stories for older children. Many are illustrated and generally they are well produced. Some contain a single Bible story, while others contain many.

Leaders may often wish to find a Bible story or suitable theme to illustrate a particular lesson subject and so the following suggestions are a rough guide which may be found helpful. Much depends on the age and ability of the children, and the theme on which you are teaching; and Sunday school lesson books usually provide Bible references for you. Parents wishing to choose a Bible story to tell may also find this list helpful.

Infants — up to approx 5 years:

OT	—The Creation	Gen 1:1–2:4
	Moses in the Bulrushes	Ex 2:1–10
	The Child Samuel	1 Sam 3:1–21
NT	—The Birth of Jesus	Lk 2:1–20
	The Wise Men	Mt 2:1–12
	The Lost Sheep	Lk 15:3–7
	Jesus heals Ten Lepers	Lk 17:11–19

Juniors — approx 5–8 years:

OT —Ruth .... Ruth 1 and 2
     Naaman, the Leper .... 2 Kings 5:1–19
     Daniel in the Lions' Den .... Dan 6:1–27
     Jonah and the Big Fish .... Jon 1:1–3:10

NT —Jesus goes to the Temple at 12 years
     old .... Lk 2:41–51
     Jesus turns Water into Wine .... Jn 2:1–11
     Jesus heals a Paralysed Man .... Mk 2:1–12
     Jesus feeds over 5,000
     people .... Jn 6:1–14; Mt 14:13–21
     Jesus calms a Storm .... Lk 8:22–25
     The Prodigal Son .... Lk 15:11–32
     Zacchaeus .... Lk 19:1–10
     The First Palm Sunday .... Mt 21:1–11
     The First Easter Day .... Jn 20:1–18

Older children — approx 8 years and over:

OT —Noah — the Ark, the Flood, and the
     Rainbow .... Gen 6:9–9:17
     Joseph and his Brothers .... Gen 37:1–36
     Joseph in Egypt .... Gen 39:1–46:7
     Crossing the Red Sea .... Ex 14:5–31
     The Fall of Jericho .... Josh 6:1–20
     Elijah and the Prophets of
     Baal .... 1 Kings 18:1–45 (or 17–45)
     The Burning Fiery Furnace .... Dan 3:1–30

NT —Jesus heals a Leper .... Mk 1:40–45
     The Sower .... Mk 4:1–20
     Blind Bartimaeus .... Mk 10:46–52
     The First Good Friday .... Mk 15:16–39
     The Walk to Emmaus on the
     first Easter night .... Lk 24:13–35
     Jesus ascends to
     Heaven .... Mt 28:16–20; and Acts 1:4–11

This list is by no means exhaustive, and there are many other Bible stories which are suitable for children.

8

Children and Questions

A The use of questions as a teaching aid

It may be thought that asking questions of children is a very simple thing which anyone can do. In some respects that may be true, but for teachers and leaders of the young there is much more in it than meets the eye (or rather the ear). To ask a question of a child we must ask it skilfully in order to draw out the answer we require. It is surprisingly easy to get an answer from a child in church or in Sunday groups which may well be a correct answer but is not the answer which was wanted.

We ask children questions when we are teaching them so that the children have to think. Usually their answers will tell us how much they have understood of what we have been trying to teach. This presupposes that we have asked the question properly and also that we have taught well. A wrong answer may not always be the fault of the child; it could be due to the teacher's inaccurate or poor teaching.

There are certain points about asking questions which, if followed, are much more likely to produce the answers which are required.

1 Good questions are clear

If you were to ask a group of children who had been hearing about St Paul the apparently simple question,

'What was Paul?' you could produce a variety of answers: he was a missionary; he was a Roman citizen; he was a tent-maker; he was a follower of Jesus; he was a writer of letters to young churches; and so on — all of which are right answers. But what were you really after? If you wanted the answer to be 'A tent-maker' then you should have asked, more specifically, 'What was Paul's trade?' The other replies you had, while not being factually wrong, were only given because the question was phrased badly. How were the children to know what answer was wanted from the way you had framed the question?

This question was once tried out on a group of teenagers who were wanting to be helpers in the Sunday school. When asked, 'What was Paul?' one of the group replied, 'Paul who?' The other members of the group laughed, but the leader said that the girl's answer was quite justified, bearing in mind the poor way in which the leader (deliberately) had asked the question.

If the question is not asked in a clear way, the children will either sit puzzling over what you want, or they will make a guess at the answer, or they will decide it is too hard for them and will sit back and hope that one of their fellows can cope.

2 Good questions are simple and direct

Ask the question simply and directly without any unnecessary words. For instance, do not put a question like this:

> I wonder whether any of you can think back to last week and tell me where Jesus was when he called his first disciples, and what they were doing when he called them, and what were the names of some of them?

This may be somewhat exaggerated, but it is an example of the rambling wordy type of question which one sometimes hears. By the time the questioner has got to the end, the children have forgotten the beginning! Why not ask the question more directly — in this case as three separate and simple questions, without any preamble: 'Where was Jesus when he called his first disciples?' (By the sea of Galilee.) 'What were they doing when he called them?' (Casting/mending their nets.) 'What were the names of some of them?' (Simon Peter, Andrew, James, John.) This can be found in Mt: 4:18–22.

Make such questions not only simple and direct, but also as short as possible. In this way, you are far more likely to get a correct answer because the children will have understood what you want.

3 Good questions vary in difficulty

This gives both slow and quicker children a chance to answer.

If the questions you ask are all fairly difficult, only the brighter and more confident children will attempt to answer. The slower ones will be apt to sit back and think, 'So-and-so will answer that so I needn't bother,' and they will probably opt out of the group mentally at that point.

But we must ensure that the slower and less able children are not left out. We should direct some of the straightforward questions especially to them, so that they feel they are taking part. This is good caring psychology. It is good to address them by name too, eg 'Perhaps Susan knows the answer to that one ... ?' having asked a question which you are fairly sure Susan can cope with. When you get a correct answer, especially from a less able child, it is important to remember to praise the child, so that he/she feels encouraged enough to want to try again.

4 Good questions do not usually require a simple 'Yes' or 'No' answer

Often children can guess, from the tone of your voice or the way you have phrased the question, whether the answer is 'Yes' or 'No', and it does not usually require much thought on their part. Such questions are not entirely unavoidable, however, and if you do have to ask a question in that way, try to follow it up with a 'Why?' or 'Why not?', so that it leads the child on to think a little more deeply.

Sometimes you may have a shy child in the group for whom a 'Yes' or 'No' answer would be quite an achievement. If so, it may not be wise to question such a child further, but to ask the rest of the group, 'Can anyone else tell me why?' It is really a point of knowing the children well so that you may frame questions which will suit their needs and capabilities.

Shyer children should have our particular care on Sundays, so that they may feel secure in the church, and know that the leader is someone to whom they can relate, and have a chance to achieve something under his care.

5 The answers to good questions are within the child's knowledge

Do not ask a question to which the child cannot possibly know the answer. This will only result in blank stares or wild guesses. If possible, lead them up to such questions by asking simpler ones first, so that they will have some knowledge on which to build the answer. When they have found out enough to be able to answer the hard question, it is then quite fair to ask it.

All these guidelines point to the fact that it is helpful to *prepare some questions beforehand*. Keep the children in mind and design some questions specifically for the less able children as well as some for the brighter ones.

To help you to plan a few questions, remember that many questions begin with the letter 'W': 'What?' 'Where?' 'Why?' 'When?' 'Who?' for instance. Another useful word to begin a question is 'How?'

Incidentally, apart from asking certain questions of particular children, it is a good general rule to make sure that *every* child in your group is referred to *by name* at least once every Sunday. This helps them to feel they belong, and they will be unlikely to go home thinking no adult has spoken to them, and that no one even noticed they were there.

B The children's answers

There are also some ways in which we can react to the children's answers in order to get the best from them:

1 Be prepared to wait for an answer

Pause to give the children time to think when you have asked your question. Some children take longer to sort out their thoughts than others and they will not get a chance to answer if you are not patient enough to give them time. If you quickly tell them the answer yourself when no immediate reply is forthcoming, then it is highly likely that the children will learn nothing from the question. They will learn much more if they have been able to work out the answer for themselves.

2 Do not always accept an answer from the first child to put up his hand

If you do, then one or two of the brighter children will do almost all of the answering. The other children will soon realise that this is happening and will either sit back and leave it all to them, or they will feel frustrated that they haven't been able to join in themselves. Either way, they will probably feel that questions are not for them.

Certainly accept the bright child's answer once or twice, but thereafter say something like, 'Yes, I expect you know, but you've had two turns so shall we see if anyone else can answer.' The bright child can always have another turn later in the session, so that he doesn't feel he can opt out after having done his bit at the beginning.

3 Make the best of all the answers given

Use even the wrong answers. Ask if another child can correct a wrong answer or add something to a partially correct one. Try not to say a discouraging 'No'. Instead, try to find something right about his answer, and encourage him to think a little bit further, possibly with another clue from you.

If no child is correct, and the answer is in the Bible, give those children who can read the reference and let them look it up and tell you.

4 Discourage flippant or careless answers

There may be a young 'humourist' in the group who enjoys giving a 'funny' answer in order to make his fellows laugh. You may smile, but you should make it clear that you were not impressed by the silly reply and you should ask the child to think again. (This does not mean that there should be no fun in the Sunday sessions!)

Much the same goes for the answer from the child who says the first thing that comes into his head without giving the question any thought. He or she should be asked to think again and give a better answer. The children need to realise that we expect the best from them all, and that we know that they can do better than merely giving flippant or careless answers.

5 Guard against the type of answer which the children feel is expected in Sunday groups and in church

Questions which include the words 'he' or 'him' are often answered on Sundays by 'God' or 'Jesus', because it is the type of answer which the children apparently feel is bound to be right! But we can usually supplement this type of answer, even if it is right, by asking a further question which requires a little more thought. For example (in Lk 19:1–10): 'Whom did Zacchaeus learn to love and follow?' (Jesus.) 'What did he do to show his love?' (Promised to give half his goods to the poor and give back four times the money he had taken by fraud.)

C When do we ask questions in church and in Sunday groups?

We ask questions especially at the following times to gain interest and to reinforce the lesson:

1 At the beginning of the session

Such questions may be of a general nature, designed to gain the child's interest and to get the whole group thinking in one direction. For example, in an Epiphany lesson about the Wise Men (in early January), you might begin with a few general questions about gifts: 'What gifts (or presents) were you given at Christmas?' (You will surely be told!) 'Which of you *gave* any gifts?' When their minds are all concentrated on gifts and giving, you might say, 'Today we are going to talk about some gifts which were given to a very special child . . '

2 During the course of the session

These questions will relate to the theme of the session, and the answers will show how well the children are understanding it. If there are any obvious gaps or mis-understandings, you will have a chance to right them before going on further. Questions during a session also help to recall any wandering minds back to the subject, especially if addressed by name to a child who is obviously not 'with you'.

3 At the end of the session

This may help to build up a summary or résumé of the lesson (perhaps on a large sheet or a blackboard). Such questions will also help to find out how much the children have taken in and how much they will carry away with them. If possible, design questions whose answers sum up the points you have been trying to teach. Then really impress the summary on them by letting them take part in some activity connected with it: drawing, writing, acting, model-making, etc. (They may already have been doing these things during the session, as activities should not always be left to the end.) If the children *do* something in connection with the session, it is more likely that they will understand the point of it and be able to re-member it. Also it may have some direct result in their lives, which is the whole aim of teaching.

D The questions children ask us

Parents and Sunday group leaders are often faced with children's questions concerning religion which are not easy to answer: 'Where is God?' 'What happens when you die?' 'How old is God?' 'Where is heaven?' and so on. Children have a habit of asking these most difficult questions at awkward or inconvenient times when the adult cannot give full attention to the matter.

However, the moment is not inconvenient for the questioner. It is all part of the child's healthy curiosity about life and a desire for knowledge. So we should not discourage questions; and we should always do our best to give an honest answer at the time the child asks, because that is the time when he is wanting to know and when he is ready to learn. If we put the child off, obviously he will feel rebuffed and will not feel satisfied. Also if we come back with the answer a few days later, he is likely to be occupied with something else, and will probably not be nearly so receptive to the answer. Children expect answers to their questions when they ask them, for adults are the fount of all knowledge in their eyes and they see no reason why they cannot have an instant and complete reply. This is somewhat daunting for the caring leader or parent but one has to do the best one can.

Whatever the circumstances, it is important that we give a truthful answer to the child's question. Half-truths or invented replies will eventually be discovered to be wrong and will lead the child to mistrust the adult who supplied the answer.

With questions about God, which may well be unanswerable by any human, we have a chance to inculcate into a child's mind a sense of awe, wonder and reverence for God. We may reply on the lines of, 'God is so wonderful and great and holy that only he knows the answer to that one. We ordinary people must just trust him.'

This may well be enough to satisfy a young questioner. None of us can hope to know anything like all the answers to questions about God, life, death and so on. If we did, we would be as great as he is, and in admitting that we don't know we have a chance to point the child's thoughts to the greatness and majesty of God who alone knows everything.

Sometimes children ask questions out of habit, as when they ask a continual series of 'But ... why?' to every reply we make. At other times they may simply be asking a question because they want to gain our attention; but most questions are genuine needs for knowledge and understanding, and it is to those that we must direct our best answers (though the others should not be answered wrongly, of course). Finding out the answers to questions is one of a child's chief ways of finding out about life.

We should also bear in mind the child's age and experience when he asks the questions. A very young child will often be satisfied with, and usually only needs, a very short simple answer. There is no point in going into a long and complicated one.

A four-year-old once asked his father, 'Where did I come from?' The father was somewhat taken aback and felt that the child was too young for the answer to such questions. However, he did his best with a rather long, if simplified answer to the question, to which the child listened in puzzled silence. At the end, he said with a worried frown, 'Well that's very funny, Daddy.' 'Why?' asked the father. 'Because Timmy, who sits next to me at the playgroup, says *he* came from Doncaster.'

Similarly, a young girl came home from school one day and asked, 'What is vice?' Her parents tried to explain, to which the child said, 'I don't know how I'm going to do all that because, you see, I've just been made Vice-captain of our form.'

Both these stories show how important it is to try to find out what the child is really wanting to know when he asks the question.

It is likewise important that our answers shall be clear

to the child. A class had been learning about St Matthew, the tax-collector, and the teacher asked the following week, 'Can you remember what St Matthew did for a living?' 'He kept a cab-rank, Sir,' answered a bright boy. As the teacher looked very puzzled, the boy went on, 'You said he collected taxis, Sir.'

Many of our answers to children's questions about God will depend on the sort of attitude and feeling we have for him ourselves. Things which we have found helpful we will naturally want to pass on to the children. Yet we will be aware that we are going on learning all the time, and cannot ever hope to 'know it all.'

It is not possible to give complete answers to the questions which children may ask about God, life and death, etc. So much depends on the circumstances, the child, his age, level of understanding, what he really wants to know, and so on. Moreover, small children are only capable of thinking in concrete images, and it is useless to expect them to understand abstract ideas.

Generally a small child will accept quite a simple answer to a question. We will probably be aware that we have not given him the whole story, but we can build on his knowledge and add to it later as the child gets older. As his knowledge and experience grows, we can help him to consult books and to think things out for himself.

Bearing all this in mind, the following guidelines may help adults to frame an answer to some of the child's big questions about the religious side of life.

Who made God?

The simple answer to this one is 'Nobody'. God has always been there from the very beginning. He was there before the world was made. He made the world and everything in it. If someone else had 'made God', he wouldn't be God. The first four words of the Bible are,

'In the beginning God ..' (Gen 1:1). Everything which exists can be traced back in its origin to God. The bread we eat comes from flour, which comes from corn, which starts as a seed, to which God gave life and growth. The farmer helped by planting the seed, watering it and so on: but he could not give it life and make it grow. Only God can give life and man cannot make as much as a single, living blade of grass.

Similarly, our woollen clothes come from wool, which comes from sheep, to which God gave life and growth. Our cotton clothes come from cotton plants, which start as tiny seeds in the cotton fields, and God made them live and grow. Many pieces of furniture are made of wood, which comes from the trees of the forest, which were caused to grow by God.

So we could go on. Everything is traceable back, ultimately, to God. The cleverest scientists in the world can come up with amazingly complex machinery, iron lungs, artificial hearts and so on, but they need the brains, given to them by God, in order to do it. Wonderful though machines are, they cannot produce life.

So, who made God? Nobody.

How old is God?

God does not have an age as we do. He never grows old because he doesn't change. He always was, always is, and always will be there — always the same, always present, though we cannot see him, and always loving to us, his children.

What is God like?

No one has ever seen God, but he sent his Son, the Lord Jesus Christ, to show us what he (God) is like, and to help us to understand. God is like Jesus: always caring, kind and loving, loving us even more than we love ourselves. He is like the very best kind of parent or strong and loving friend you can think of — and much more than that. 'He who has seen me has seen the Father,' said Jesu to Philip, one of his disciples, when he was explaining what God the Father is like (Jn 14:9). Although no one has seen God, we do have some idea, through Jesus, of what he is like.

Where is God?

The simple answer to this is 'everywhere', but we shall probably need to enlarge on it in order to satisfy a curious child. We might begin by suggesting that if we turn out all the lights in the room, the child will know that his parents are still 'there', loving him, even though he cannot see them. He will still know that their love is there, even if he is in another room in the house, or even if he is away staying with his grandmother. That love is still 'with him', and will be wherever he goes.

It is a little like that with God. Our human eyes cannot see him yet we know he is there. 'How?' might well be the next question. Ask the child how, by simply looking out of the window, he can tell whether or not it is a windy day. He can see what the wind does — blows trees about, blows the washing on the line, and so on — but can he see the wind itself? No.

Similarly, we cannot see God but we know he is everywhere because all around us are the things which he is doing. The sun gives us light, and even when we cannot see the sun itself, we still have the light. We have beautiful sunsets, the stars and the moon, clouds, trees, flowers, cuddly pets, kind and loving people — in fact everything in the world which is good.

You can't see love, but you can 'feel' it and know it is there by the things which people do and the kind ways in which they speak and act.

In the same way, when we see or feel something good or lovely, then we are feeling that God is near because everything that is good comes from him. So God is everywhere, all about us. A Girl Guide leader said that she encouraged her Guides to spell God with two 'o's' (GOOD), and this is a helpful pointer to our understanding of him.

God is not limited as we are; he is not only in one place at one time, as our human bodies limit us; he is everywhere all the time. Jesus showed this when, after the Resurrection, he was able to appear in the midst of his friends and join in the conversation as though he had been with them all the time — as indeed he had, but not visibly.

Jesus also said that God knows whenever one tiny sparrow falls to the ground. He also even knows how many hairs we have on our heads (Mt 10:29–30). Because he can be everywhere and see everything at every moment, he is able to be with everyone all over the world at the same time.

If we find this hard to imagine, then it is because we are only human. If we could fully understand it, we would be as great as God.

Where is heaven?

We need to keep away from the 'above the bright blue sky' idea, as is suggested in some hymns, when we answer this one.

Heaven is not thought of so much as a place but as a state. One parent once said to a child, 'Heaven is where God is, just as home is where Mum and Dad are.' It is misleading to suggest that heaven is 'up there' or 'beyond the sky', though that in one sense is true. But heaven is not only there; it is much more than that.

To an older child who has this 'up there' idea, we

might point out that when he went 'up' a class in school, he did not necessarily go up on to a higher floor. 'Up' in that sense means 'different, better'. Heaven is certainly 'up' in the sense that it is better than this world, something we may 'look up to'; and in the sense that it is 'above' it is helpful to think of it as 'above (or beyond) our present understanding'.

While heaven may certainly be 'up there', it is also 'down here', around us all the time — because God is everywhere.

How do you know there is a heaven if you can't see it?

Jesus told us there was. He taught us to pray, 'Our Father, who art in heaven . .' He also talked about God as 'our heavenly Father'. He told us lots of stories (parables) to show us what the kingdom of heaven is like (Mt 13:24–52). Because he is Jesus, we know that we can believe and trust him, and so we know that what he said is true.

We do not have to see everything in order to believe it. I 'know' that there is a land called Iceland, although I have never been there; but I have seen books about it and heard talks given by experts who have been there. Because I know that they know far more about it than I do, then I am happy to trust that what they say is right. Similarly, I trust and accept all that Jesus told us about heaven.

What are angels?

Angels are God's messengers. There are lots of stories in the Bible of angels bringing people messages from God. For instance, an angel came to tell Mary that she would have a son who would be Jesus (Lk 1:26–38); an angel told the woman at the tomb that Jesus had risen from the dead (Mt 28:1–8); angels came to Jesus after he had been tempted in the wilderness (Mt 4:1–11). There are several references to angels in various parts of the Bible, for instance: Ps 91:11; Mt 25:31; Mt 26:53; Lk 15:10. Sometimes they appeared in shining white clothes, such as in Mt 28:2–3; sometimes they appeared to people in dreams, as in Mt 2:19.

People do not become angels when they die; angels are a different order of being. Also they are real, not like fairies who are 'pretend' people in stories. (We must beware that children do not mix the two, otherwise when they get too big for fairy stories, they may well give up believing that angels exist too.)

If a child has been to the Holy Communion Service and is old enough to understand something of what is being said in the service, we could point out that we are worshipping with the angels when we praise God and say,

> 'Therefore with angels and archangels,[7] and with all the company of heaven, we proclaim your great and glorious name . .'[8]

When we see pictures of angels with wings (or pictures of doves or tongues of fire, or any other biblical image), we should take care to tell children that this is how the artist imagined it. Then we might ask, 'How would *you* draw an angel [or whatever the image is representing]?' Children often show remarkable powers of getting hold of the real point. They may have a depth of understanding and insight which is better than (certainly different from) ours, for a child is often closer to the spiritual realm than we realise. Therefore we must not ignore their ideas and images. To discuss them may well help both child and adult.

What is the Holy Spirit?

The Holy Ghost or Holy Spirit is the Spirit of God. 'Ghost' is the same in meaning as 'Spirit', and both refer to the third person of the Holy Trinity. After Jesus had gone back to heaven at his ascension, on the Day of Pentecost (or Whitsunday), he sent the Holy Spirit to the disciples to give them power and strength to continue his work in the world. The Holy Spirit is very much at work in the world today. He comes to us when we put our trust in God, and is with everyone who believes, wherever they may be.

Sometimes he is called 'the Comforter', and 'comfort' in this sense means to 'strengthen' and to give consolation, rather than the 'cushion' idea of comfort.

The Holy Spirit comes to guide and strengthen us in life and helps us in our service of God. Our part is to ask for his help and to trust that we will receive it. He is also helping us through our consciences when we know inside ourselves that we must not do the wrong thing which we are being tempted to do.

Likewise, he is guiding and strengthening us when we feel that we must do or say something which is right and good — because everything that is good in the world comes from God.

Are God and Jesus and the Holy Spirit three people joined together?

Not in the literal sense. They are all one God; but God is so wonderful that he has given us three ways in which to know and understand him. To help us to see what that means, think of your mother: she is mother to you, she is wife to your father, and she is daughter to your grandmother. But she is not *three* separate people; she is *one* person. This in a very simple, inadequate way, helps us with our thinking about God. He is:

1 God the Father, the Creator, who made all the world and everything in it;

2 God the Son, Jesus Christ, who came to this earth and lived and died and rose again for us, and showed us what God is like;

3 God the Holy Spirit, who guides and strengthens us, and from whom come all good words and thoughts and deeds.

Questions about death

Since death comes to every family sooner or later, it is something about which children will have many questions which are not always easy to answer. Nonetheless, small children often accept death more easily than do many adults, although they are still likely to ask us difficult questions about it.

A six-year-old child whose mother had died of cancer came up to her Sunday school teacher with a bright smile and said, all in one breath, 'My mummy's dead and we are going to Canada!' She seemed far less perturbed than the teacher (who had been worrying about what to say to her which would be of the greatest comfort), and had apparently accepted the fact of her mother's death in the normal course of events. She was, of course, too young to realise all the implications at the time.

Even so, when Granny or Aunt Jane dies, there is bound to be a gap in the family — a gap which puzzles children and one which adults often find difficult to talk about. This is particularly so if the adults were close to the person who has died, and so are suffering from the strains of grief themselves.

Children's questions on this, as on any other serious topic, need an answer and probably a discussion too. So we have to be prepared to talk about the loss of Granny or whoever, difficult though that may be if we were close to the person concerned. A clergyman or leader will doubtless find such a conversation easier than a parent. But if the person who has died was close to us too, then we should remember that children may not feel the trauma in the same way in which we do, and this is especially so in the case of very young children.

Another point to remember is that children to a large extent take their attitudes from the adults around them. If the bereaved adults are excessively tearful, the children will be upset because their parents (or whoever it is) are upset — not mainly because of the loss of Granny. However if the parents show no sign of sadness at all, the children may be equally confused! Talking with children and seeing their matter-of-fact outlook can, in fact, be a help to adults in coping with personal grief.

But what about trying to answer the children's natural questions? As we have said earlier, very young children are often satisfied with short and simple answers, and we may well not have to give them a great amount of detail.

The following thoughts may help, although much depends on the individual child, his age and temperament, etc, so that it is not possible to give a stereotyped answer which will suit in all cases.

Why did Granny have to die?

In the case of death after an illness, it may be that we can suggest that God knew that Granny was in a lot of pain and would never be well enough to enjoy life here as she once did; so he took her to live with him, where she will have no more aches and pains and where she will be much, much happier than anyone can be on earth. Although we won't be seeing her for a while, we haven't lost her for ever because God is looking after her, and he has planned that one day we will all meet again. (If we can say this while looking happy at the prospect, then it

will help to comfort a child who is sensing the loss deeply
— as some children do.)

How can Granny be with God when she is buried in the churchyard?

This question may come from an older child, perhaps one who was old enough to go to the funeral. The answer is that it is only Granny's body which is buried in the churchyard — not the real Granny who loved us and whom we love. We are all made up of a body (which we can see) and a soul or spirit (which we cannot see), and the soul is the real person and it has not died.

The body may get old, worn out or ill, and so it is finished with and cast away, like an old coat which is no longer needed. The soul, the real person, goes on living somewhere where our eyes cannot see. We do not know exactly where this is, but we can leave the matter safely in God's care. He loves us so much that we know that Granny will be very happy with him.

Much of the evidence for this comes from the Bible, and especially from the things Jesus told us and the things which he did. (Rising from the dead himself, and raising others — Lazarus (Jn 11:1–44), and the widow's son at Nain (Lk 7:11–17) for instance.)

The fact that we cannot 'prove' that there is life after death for ourselves — at least not while we are still here on earth — is no reason why we should not believe it. We accept the sayings of the experts on other subjects, even though we may not be able to 'prove' them in a scientific sense, and so we accept this great fact of ever-lasting life too.

How did Granny's soul get out of her body?

Perhaps in rather the same way that our mind gets out of our body when we think about somewhere else or when we dream. The soul is not another part of the body which we can touch as we can touch our head or our foot or our hand, but it is a real part of us. The soul is the *real person*, while the body is just the shape it takes while it is here on earth. The soul is not something which could be photographed, but it is the 'you' that thinks and feels and loves.

When a caterpillar turns into a beautiful butterfly, it does not become a different being; it is simply the same being, but in a different form. So, when we die, although we may have a different sort of 'look' to us (though we do not know exactly what sort of a 'look' that will be), we will still be the same person inside.

Will Granny miss us like we miss her?

Granny will be with God and she will not be suffering any pain any more. She will be very happy, and she will almost certainly know about us and know that God is still looking after us. Although we cannot help but miss her, we know that she would not want us to be miserable. She would want us to go on doing the things we did with her and which made her happy. Perhaps we could still do the same sort of things with Auntie so-and-so? Then that would make her happy too. Granny may then know that some good has come out of her not being with us.

Dying is not the worst thing that can happen to us, because it is not the end of everything. It is the beginning of a new sort of life for the one who has died — a far better and happier life than the one here on earth if that person believes and trusts in Jesus.

Will my puppy go to heaven when he dies?

God made all the animals, including your puppy, and he wants us to look after and take care of them; you do this by feeding Fido, brushing him and taking him for walks. God cares for everything he has made, and while we do not know where Fido will go when he dies, we can certainly trust God to look after him when that happens.

It is hoped that these thoughts might be of some use to leaders, parents and others who have to cope with a death in the family when children want explanations. We cannot possibly provide all the answers, and it is right that we admit as much and throw the child's thoughts back to the wonder and greatness of the only one who does know all the answers — GOD. If, through this, we can induce the right sort of sense of awe and trust in a child's mind, then our discussions and answers will have achieved something which is bound to help.

Why do people have to suffer?

This is a question which might be asked by an older child as a corollary to the questions about death. We may reply that we all suffer — and gain — from the things which other people do. Often (but not always) tragedies which cause suffering may be traced back to someone's negligence or wrong-doing. No one can live entirely to himself, and we all not only suffer from people's errors but also gain from their wisdom, skills, and kindnesses.

If an illness or an accident cannot be traced back in this way, then we may tell a child that, because we are only human, there are many things which we do not know. Only God knows all the answers, and until we meet him in the after-life we must continue to trust him, for, whatever happens, we can be sure that he knows best.

Why does God let people do wrong things, like murdering and mugging, etc?

In his wisdom God gave us all free-will, the freedom to do right or wrong, to choose good or bad, and it is by using these choices that we develop character. There would be no virtue in doing good if we were all made like robots and were unable to do anything other than the correct thing every time because we were 'programmed' that way. We would never learn anything.

We do not always guard and protect our children from every possible harm or mistake that could hurt them. We know that they have to learn to cope with life, and so sometimes we have to let them take some risks so that they may discover some truths for themselves. We know that in this way they will be learning to cope with and triumph over difficulties, so that in the end they may grow into sturdy and independent characters.

So we cannot blame God when people murder or mug people or steal or commit any other of the sins which we have been warned against. God has given us the choice and, loving Father that he is, it makes him sad when people choose wrong and so harm their own lives and cause suffering and unhappiness to others.

Is there a real Father Christmas?

Older children sometimes try to disabuse younger ones of their belief in Father Christmas. 'It's only Daddy dressed up,' they'll scoff. Then the little one protests, 'But I *saw* him in the store! Can't I stay up tonight and see him so that I'll *know* he's real?'

When should we tell a child the truth? The moment of disillusionment is bound to come sooner or later, but how can we tell them without upsetting their confidence too much? We need to beware that when they decide the story is only for babies, they do not also cast aside the *real* Christmas story of the birth of Jesus with it.

However, if we tell them the legend of Santa Claus, based on a real person, it is likely that they may get the best of both worlds.

The origins of the story are a little obscure, but in the fourth century there lived a Bishop of Myra in Asia Minor. His name was Nicholas, and he is thought to have been imprisoned for his faith. Many legends grew up around him, and one stressed his kindness and how he used to go about leaving gifts for the poor and needy, often anonymously.

In one case he heard of three sisters who were very poor and who wished to be married. On three nights he went and tossed a bag of gold into their window and hurried away, not wanting to be seen. On the third night, however, the girls' father was hiding so that he might find out who their kind friend was. When he caught him, he found to his surprise that it was the saintly Nicholas.

Later people began giving presents to their children on the eve of St Nicholas' Day (6th December). The custom spread from Europe to America and to Britain, and was eventually transferred here to Christmas Eve.

So began the custom of people copying the good St Nicholas and giving presents secretly at Christmas. One boy, hearing the story remarked, 'It's like being a secret agent! Couldn't *we* be Santa Claus to somebody?'

Thus there was a Saint Nicholas who liked to give gifts without being seen himself, and people have followed his example ever since. It is an excellent way of making other people happy; so it is real enough. It is just another name for the kindly giving which wants nothing in return.

Quite a number of churches are dedicated to the name of St Nicholas, many in seaports as he is also the patron saint of sailors, as well as of children, pawnbrokers and merchants. We might draw the children's attention to any such buildings, so enhancing the reality of St Nicholas.

We might also point out that the first and greatest ever Christmas gift was God's gift of his Son Jesus to the world.

9

Children Outside the Church and those on the Fringes

In our efforts to bring the children with whom we already have some contact into a closer relationship with God, we must not forget all those children who only have minimal contact with the church or who have none at all. They need the gospel of Christ just as much as 'church' children.

According to the General Synod Board of Education's report *Children in the Way* (1988), baptism statistics suggest that 'the Church of England has accepted pastoral and catechetical responsibility for over one-third of the child population, or some 2,881,000 infants, children and young people under the age of 14.'[9]

Of these the Church has further contact on Sundays with some 393,000 infants and children up to the age of 13.[10] There are also around 114,000 up to 13-year-olds in youth groups and church choirs, and involved as servers and bell-ringers.[11]

These figures point to the fact that we should be doing more to attract more children into the church — difficult and complex though that operation often is.

In some churches it may be possible to make more contact with the uniformed organisations in the parish, such as Scouts, Guides, Cubs, Brownies, Boys' Brigade, Girls' Brigade, Church Lads' and Church Girls' Brigade. According to the *Children in the Way* report this would involve some 341,000 more children.[12]

While some of such children may appear at church parades, perhaps once a month or so, they may not get a great deal more Christian teaching unless they are blessed with Christian leaders. It may be possible to meet the leaders, with a view to arranging that the organisations take a greater part in the life of the church. The children might be invited to attend Family Services (and to bring their families) and some of them may take an active part in the services; the organisations may be invited to have a share in other church events — helping at bazaars, fêtes, decorating a part of the church for festivals, designing some of the posters, and so on. The clergy may perhaps visit the organisations at their own meetings on occasions — and all of this will help the young folk to see that they are a valued part of the church community.

What of all the countless thousands of children with whom the church has very tenuous contact — the children whose only appearance is at their baptism, those in the playgroup in the church hall, the mother-and-toddler group and so on, not forgetting those with whom there is no contact at all?

This is an enormous problem and it can only be tackled in small ways at a time. The most effective resources for Christian education and nurture are the human ones: people who care and whose hearts are in the welfare of those children. The church needs to demonstrate its practical concern for such children, not simply by preaching and lecturing, but by doing. It is rightly said that actions speak louder than words.

When the needs of the area have been assessed it may be found that the best way forward for the church is to provide, for example, a holiday for disadvantaged children and their families, or to start a coffee bar to keep youngsters off the streets, or to organise a week-night activity for younger children. It may also be possible to start a group for the parents of newly baptised babies and those whose children attend the playgroup. It might be that a special children's mission is needed (on the lines of the beach missions run by the Church Army); to this, each church-connected child could be invited to bring a friend who does not attend any church. Care must be taken not to bring in children whose families already belong to another church or faith, and that in all cases the parents are aware of where their children are going. There may be many children whose families have no connection with any faith at all, simply because the parents do not see that religion has any relevance for them. It is not easy for such children to accept a faith when they receive no parental support or backing, and we need to tread carefully lest we be accused of forcing children into a way of life which their families do not accept.

Where 'church children' are encouraged to bring another child — and where that child's family has no objection — then it will be a practical lesson to the church child in understanding and sharing the faith. Religion is 'caught rather than taught', it has been said, and in these ways the children outside the church and their families may gain a better understanding of what Christianity is about. We must help them to see that Christianity does not mean only going to church; it also means doing something about the way one lives and the things one says or does.

It is important that we approach the whole question of children outside the church carefully, so that we find the way which will suit the particular situation in our area. We must approach the problem with open minds and not be frightened of experimenting. What works well in one area does not necessarily work in the same way in another. Much depends on the people involved and the environment which we create for the children so that they will grow in the faith. The Christian faith means growing and learning — for us all — and the whole family of God must be seen as a true family learning from one another and helping one another.

We are not only ministering to the children, for the church has a ministry to the whole family. The backing and support of the parents helps us to nurture the children in the best possible way.

The Bible sets great emphasis on families. Most parents today are interested to know about the groups which their children join. Some parents have no idea what the Christian faith is about, and it may be that groups of dedicated lay people could visit some of the children's families, thus forging links which will be of great benefit to both the children and their parents. If we can get the interest, and eventual commitment, of the parents, we are more than halfway to attracting the children. The converse works too, for in many cases it is the children who have first brought the parents to the church.

Visitors going out to families will need some training, and this might be possible on a deanery basis with someone to advise from the Diocesan Board of Education. It is helpful too if visitors can each have something to take when they go to a family. This might only be a letter explaining what is done in the children's work of the area, or even a copy of the church magazine, together with an invitation to join some appropriate group. Nearly all parents like nothing better than to talk about their children, and if the visitor shows an interest in the child, then the family will not reject him.

10

Belonging Together

Belonging to the church together, coming to its services and events with the children included, is a sure sign that adults are taking the business of religious upbringing of the young seriously — as seriously as caring parents take the education of the children's minds and the care of their bodies. We must aim to see that not only parents but also the rest of the congregation are committed and involved in a similar way.

One often hears people say that the children of today are the church of tomorrow. This is a completely mistaken concept, for the children are very much the church of *today*. Some members of the congregation do not realise the contribution which children can make to the life of the church today nor how necessary they are for the church to have a full family life. Parents and all the rest of the worshipping community need to show positively that they accept and welcome children as fellow members of Christ's body. We must all help them to feel that they really do belong *now* — not that they must wait until they are grown up. All members of the church, of whatever age, need to grow in their relationship with God and with one another.

At the end of a church service one may see a kindly member of the congregation talking to another member — perhaps an older one — and enquiring after their health. But how often does one see an adult speaking to a child in a similar friendly fashion? Most children probably come out of a church service feeling that no one, apart from their own family (if present), even noticed they were there. No wonder they often declare that church is boring. It is also not surprising that children feel that church and the 'learning about God' process (which is how they see Sunday school) is something which they can cast off when they reach the teenage years, for the adults seem quite ignorant of their presence and apparently themselves do not go on learning once they have left Sunday school. If, however, the children feel part of the congregation and see that adults are going on learning too, then they are far more likely to want to stay within the worshipping community.

As a beginning to accepting the children, it would be quite a simple matter for adults to acknowledge the younger members of God's family, so that when they meet them outside the church, they can greet the child by name. One only needs to ask a child's name and perhaps which school he attends to be able to greet him with a friendly, 'Hello, Tim', for example, whenever one sees him.

We say at the ASB Baptism Service that we *welcome* the child, but most of us do not do very much about it! As the children get older, they will no doubt come to recognise at least some of the church congregation when they see them outside church premises, but if those adults do not speak to the children, then the children will not get a very sanguine idea of the church family as the family of God.

In human families we do not ignore or simply tolerate the children in most of the things we do, for it is rightly felt that we are all dependent on one another. The whole family joins in many of our activities — each according

to his ability — and this should also be true of the family
of God.

When children say that 'church is boring', are they not
really saying that they don't feel welcome there and they
don't feel they belong? Surely this is something which
can be remedied by all adults welcoming and accepting
children into the church family without any conditions.

In the Church Missionary Society's magazine *Yes*
for July/September 1981, the former Children's Work
Adviser, the Revd Ivor Hughes, tells of a visit to a
church where he had been asked to preach and where
there were some 40 youngsters from various uniformed
organisations present. The local clergyman had not previously mentioned them and when Mr Hughes asked
about them, he was told, 'We don't bother with them,
they just bring the flags.' In another church Mr Hughes
was told not to bother about the children present as 'we
get rid of them after the first hymn.' What an appalling
attitude to the younger members of our church family! Is
it any wonder that we don't keep children in the church
when they are treated like this? Fortunately, this does
not appear to be a very general attitude these days, and
one hopes that there are only a few unhappy places
where such conditions still exist.

To look at the other side of the picture, in another
church Mr Hughes was fascinated to hear that at one
point in the service it was the adults who went out
into the vestry for their prayers and sermon, while the
children split up into groups around the church itself
because they outnumbered the adults. Obviously the
children felt welcomed in that parish.

If the church is to live as a true family, then we will
have to work out ways in which we can share our various
skills and ideas. We will need to include everybody in
our plan, from the youngest children (who learn from

imitating their elders) to the oldest adults (who will have much from experience to contribute). In this 'family concept' we must be careful not to leave out single people and those who live alone. If they are without a human family, then they are still very much part of God's family, the church. One lady whose own children were grown-up was heard to say that she didn't go to the Family Services in her parish any more as she felt such things were not now for her.

So wherever possible we must not segregate the members of God's family into separate groups — though there will still be occasions when such divisions are right and necessary — but we will need to look for as many times as possible when things can be done together.

Learning all together

For too long churches have operated in too many separate compartments for too much of the time — Sunday school, youth club, Young Wives, Mothers' Union, Men's Society, and so on — and hardly ever have they met together as members of God's family in that place, apart from Sunday services. The chances to get to know one another in such a situation are indeed slight.

There is often a great gap between adults and today's children. The children of this late twentieth century have far more choices and are subjected to far greater pressures than their parents were when they were young. Children today are exposed to much media advertising, to the supposed 'joys' of such things as cigarettes, alcohol and drugs, and to peer pressure ('Everybody does it so it must be all right'). The church must take these things into account; it must listen to children to understand what their problems and concerns are — some children are seriously concerned about issues such as drugs, unemployment and so on, and they need adult backing to help them deal with such problems. Within this context, the church must find ways in which both children and adults can grow, share, and also worship together. We should review our church services and events, and ask ourselves which of these can best help the young and what there is which we can all do together, for the church is the one and only organisation which is open to everybody, from the youngest to the oldest inhabitant, and in which everybody is welcome.

Learning is a process which should be seen within the context of the church as a Christian community — not merely something which happens in watertight compartments for the young on a Sunday. Children do not stop learning when they leave school; neither should adults stop learning about God when they become too old for Sunday school. In the Christian life learning goes on for ever, for we can never know all there is to know about our great and glorious Godhead. One of the ways in which adults in the church presently go on learning is through sermons. Often the sermon is seen as the only learning vehicle for them. But there are many other ways in which adults and children can learn. Children are not only learning when they are sitting in a classroom and are being told something; in fact, the chances are that if they are only listening, they are probably not learning very much. They are likely to be learning a lot more from things they see and from things they do. They are also learning all the time from their surroundings and from the actions of people in them and from their own experiences. Much the same is true of adults but we do not apply that truth very often to learning about God.

One way which will help adults and children to learn together more, is if they can all be learning about the same subject at the same time — even if some of the age-group learning has to be in separate places. This enables families to get together when they get home after church and to discuss and share their learning experiences from the things that have happened in their own group — assuming the groups have been separated.

Some useful material has been produced to help in this process: Scripture Union (130 City Road, London, EC1V 2NJ) produces *Learning All Together* magazines, which give teaching material and children's 'take-home' leaflets for the '5–7s', the '7–11s', and the '11–14s', together with suggestions for adult sermon material linked with them for the day — all on the same theme. There is also a course and children's leaflets for the '3–5s', but this does not generally follow the more adult themes.

The Church Information Office (Church House Publishing, Church House Bookshop, 31 Great Smith Street, London, SW1P 3BN) publishes *Share the Word* and *Share the Word 2* (The Wadderton Group) which provides a Sunday-by-Sunday course for all ages in the worshipping community. There are vivid, lively sessions linked to everyday experiences and there are alternative ideas for younger and older children.

The National Christian Education Council (Robert Denholm House, Nutfield, Redhill, Surrey, RH1 4HW) has *Partners in Learning*, which is designed for the whole church community and gives resource material for local churches, junior churches, ministers and ecumenical teams. They include all-age activities as well as separate age-range material and Activity Papers for the children.

In choosing our material, obviously a knowledge of the Bible is very important as we all need to know the basis for the tenets of our faith. But we also need to ask whether our sessions are giving the children any real experience of what the Christian religion is all about as it applies to them today. We need to devise activities where old and young can work side by side, each learning from their experiences. We must not look on learning simply as an intellectual experience which is connected mainly with the young.

In the worship in our churches it helps if some of the music, readings and prayers can be undertaken by different people, while the teaching can be at times all together and at times in separate groups. Some of the activities can also be undertaken by all ages together. Some parents might enjoy helping the children to make, for instance, a model of the Temple (in a theme on worship, particularly Jewish worship), while other adults might help in dressing up for acting sessions (when learning about how people lived in Bible times).

There might also be discussion groups of mixed ages when everyone has the opportunity to contribute something if they wish. One of the adults might write down the results of the discussion, not forgetting to include some of the ideas contributed by the children, which is a thing much to be encouraged. If some members of the group do not wish to say anything, then they must feel no compulsion to do so; they will probably learn much merely from listening to the discussion, and may feel encouraged to join in at a subsequent session.

Even if age groups are separated at some times, it is still possible for the whole church to work together. For instance, on Remembrance Sunday the children in one church were taken out to separate groups for the quieter and more solemn part of the service. The leader decided they should still have the opportunity to understand something of what Remembrance was all about. She felt the children ought to have the experience of 'silence' — something they seldom experience in our noisy world today. She, therefore, explained what the people in church were thinking about and then suggested that the children in their worship should have a silence too. She felt there was no great hope of success, as the youngest children were only three years old, but, to her surprise, complete silence was maintained for about one and a half minutes without there being any sound from the children.

Many churches which do not have all-age learning sessions as a regular thing might like to start off by having an all-together session occasionally, perhaps once or twice per year, so that all parts of the church family can learn together and be seen to be together at least at those times. In the Anglican Church it might be that a first-time all-age learning session could be tried on a deanery basis, or with any group of churches working together, and meeting for that occasion, perhaps on a Saturday. The diocese might also have an all-age day in the cathedral, as has been tried in several cathedrals and with great success. The idea can then be copied on a smaller scale in the parishes. There can be no hard-and-fast rules for such sessions; one has to experiment and find out what best suits the particular church or churches involved.

The *Children in the Way* report (page 91) recommends that PCCs should plan at least one venture in the year when children and adults can learn and explore together what it means to be followers 'in the Way', and should develop a continuing pattern for learning together.

Further ideas for learning apart from the Sunday sessions

Holiday clubs

These usually last for a week (or a few days) and take place during the school holidays. Though geared mainly for the children, they involve much adult participation, and parents and other members of the congregation can gain much from taking part; at the very least they will get to know some of the children better.

A holiday club usually lasts from about 10.30 am to 4 pm on the days it operates; participants bring their own picnic lunches while the church provides the drinks. A theme is chosen, which the children explore and develop through all sorts of activities which are not normally possible during the more restricted Sunday sessions.

As many adults as possible should be included, each having a particular job for one or more days; thus no one need feel committed for the whole of the period of the club, which many adults would find difficult to do. These adults may act as team leaders, scorers, games organisers, handicraft helpers, drama helpers, catering officers, registrars, collectors of money (since it is usually necessary to make a small charge to cover expenses), and even buttoners-up-of-coats and general minders for the youngest children. As many older members of the congregation as possible should also be members of the teams in the team games. This will help the children to get to know the adults.

The week may include an outing one afternoon to a local beauty spot, zoo or park, with a picnic tea and games, if the site is suitable. This may well be held on the last day of the holiday club, which will usually be the Saturday. The final event will be the church service on the Sunday, when the work which the children have done during the week can be on display and the theme of the service can be on the same lines as that of the holiday club. Some of the children may help to decorate the church with their charts, pictures, models, collages, etc on the previous Saturday morning. They could also be responsible for the church flowers on that day.

If a goodly number of adults are involved in holiday

clubs, then such events will be regarded as events for the whole church family and not just for the children alone.

Away-days or weekends

Older children, confirmation candidates and adults usually get the most out of this type of activity, but that does not mean that younger children should be excluded. A great deal can be learnt by all ages by being together for twenty-four or forty-eight hours, and whole families should certainly not be discouraged from joining in.

A suitable hotel in the off-season or a diocesan conference centre are likely venues, though it should be made clear that people are not being invited simply to a conference, or some would be put off. A youth hostel is a cheaper possibility, where younger members could join together to do chores, and perhaps relieve their elders! The adults in turn might plan some special treat for the young people.

The programme should be a mixture of recreation and learning in a relaxed atmosphere which is not too rigid. Apart from games, walks, and just chatting together, there might be a suitable film-strip or video, or a discussion, quiz, or Any Questions panel. There might also be an epilogue at the end of the day, to which people may come if they wish (they should not be pressurised); and if the away-period includes a Sunday, a service would be arranged, if there was no local church near enough for the people to attend.

The main idea of the whole away-period is to get to know youngsters and adults away from the restrictions of their normal environment, and to help all to see that they belong *together* in the family of God.

Bookstalls

At many of the events suggested in this chapter, it is useful to include a bookstall of Christian books — such as are not often seen in the High Street bookshops. For the teachers and leaders present, there might also be some resource and project materials for sale too.

If a reasonable number of people are likely to attend, then a nearby Christian bookshop will doubtless be delighted to send books, etc on sale or return, or maybe will be prepared to send someone to man the stall at certain times.

Other ideas for integrating children into the life of the whole church.

If the junior church is not to be considered as a separate entity, then obviously the congregation must be shown what it is doing and their co-operation be invited. While many parents come to church with their children, there are sadly some who do not, and these parents must not be forgotten in our efforts to get co-operation.

One way of interesting parents is to see that *some of the work of the Sunday groups goes into the homes*. If the children have done drawings or have gained achievement cards or certificates, or have been given a weekly stamp, then these are obvious examples to take home and show to the family. In telling their parents about such things, the children will in all probability be reinforcing in their own minds what they have just learnt as well as letting the parents see what has been happening.

On Mothering Sunday the children will probably take home at least a Mothering Sunday card, if not also a few flowers or a piece of simnel cake. Simnel cake proves very popular, baked by the teachers, leaders and any other willing volunteers beforehand, cut into small pieces and wrapped in foil, ready for the children to give to mother with their cards. If there is sufficient cake, other pieces may be given by the children to any grandmothers, aunts or other ladies in the congregation, and this will be much appreciated.

On Palm Sunday the children may take home a palm cross and perhaps a leaflet explaining the church's services in Holy Week and over Easter.

If the children are *learning a new hymn or a prayer*, have it duplicated or photocopied (providing you are not infringing copyright) and let each child take one home. If the parents then help the children to learn it, they will themselves be learning something which the young have been doing, and will be able to see what the children are learning about God.

It should also be remembered that if children are *taking any part in a service* (reading, leading a prayer or acting as sidesmen, for example), most parents will want to come and see or hear them.

Letters to Parents — When a new child joins the junior church, it is helpful to give or send the parents a letter saying that the church is pleased to welcome so-and-so into the Sunday group, and explaining briefly what facilities exist for the young at the church (crèche for babies, weekday meeting for children, youth groups, etc), and whether there are Family Services, pram clubs or other additions to normal Sunday groups. It is useful to have a stock of these letters duplicated, with blanks left for the name of the child and parents, so that they can be addressed individually and handed out on the day a new child arrives. Giving out such letters promptly prevents anyone complaining that their child had been going to the church for six weeks before anyone even noticed him!

It is also useful to send regular letters to all parents, say two or three times a year, giving them details of any forthcoming junior church or whole church events, such as special services, new programmes in the Sunday groups, the Christmas party, Nativity play, summer outing, and so on.

It is far better to send out such letters than to expect the children to deliver messages verbally; partly because it keeps the church in touch with the parents, and partly because children are apt to forget or get the message a bit garbled, so that the parents do not really know what is happening.

Inviting church officials into the children's groups — it is helpful to both sides if officials, such as the church warden, the treasurer, the organist, etc, can come into the Sunday groups occasionally and tell the children about their job in the church and answer questions about it, thus helping not only the young, but also the officials to see each other's life and work in the church.

Taking Part in Holy Communion — Children might be included in the offertory procession, perhaps bringing up a representative sample of the work done in their groups, in order to offer it to God. Some of the older children who have good speaking voices might occasionally lead the intercessions, including some which they have written themselves.

Adults might also be invited to come to the Sunday groups after the service to view the work which the children had been doing. If adults show interest in this way — and it takes very little effort — then the children will be greatly encouraged.

A Parents' and Leaders' Association (PLA) — This kind of group, run on similar lines to the schools' Parent/ Teachers' Association is very useful, where parents and children's leaders can join for discussions, to hear talks, or simply meet socially to talk about the children. Subjects for talks, for example, may include: Teaching children to pray; The essentials of a good home; Bringing small children to church; Orphaned and unwanted children; Coping with difficult children; Disabled children; and so on. The Diocesan RE Adviser or equivalent will no doubt be able to supply a list of suitable speakers and topics.

Not only parents of Sunday groups' children should be invited to such meetings, but also parents of choirboys and girls and of babies recently baptised. The main object is to get the parents more interested in the religious upbringing of their children and thereafter to keep their lively co-operation. The PLA might be run by a small committee whose members could serve for, say, two years, thus giving everyone a turn if they wished to help.

The PLA might also run a garden party, at which all parents could be asked to help — to run stalls, organise teas and games for the children, erect stalls, tents, and so on. Parents who may be shy of coming to church might well come to a garden party, especially if invited to have a specific part in it. Having then met the children's leaders and other church people socially, the different parents might decide that church-goers weren't quite as odd as they had thought!

An exhibition to which parents and members of the congregation can be invited is another possible ice-breaker. The PCC should also be asked to support the event by their presence. Children's work can be displayed and there might be some stage items. Refreshments might be served by some of the older children, who will no doubt be delighted to take part and thus feel that they really belong.

The exhibition can also show methods of learning,

books and equipment used, and thus dispel any views that junior church is a dull place where children do nothing more than read the Bible verse by verse.

Beyond the local church

Visiting other churches

We need to help children to realise that other churches exist besides their own. Taking a group of children to visit another church (not necessarily of one's own denomination) can be very rewarding. This might happen on a summer Saturday, and if it is combined with a picnic, it makes a doubly enjoyable outing. The visit can be made by public transport, private cars, cycles or walking, and parents should be invited to come along whenever possible.

Always write or get in touch with the minister beforehand, not only as a simple courtesy, but also because there may be a wedding or other function on which would prevent you gaining access. If you are a fairly large party it may be possible for someone to give you a conducted tour of the church, or it may be that a short service could be arranged while you are there.

Any artists or photographers might like to make a pictorial record of the visit (if permitted), and the resulting pictures could be displayed to your home congregation.

The church's magazine or history may be available at a small charge, and there may be books or leaflets for sale, which the children should be encouraged to look at, if not to buy.

If the church is collecting for any particular cause, your children might be asked if they would like to contribute, no matter how small their offering. If they understand to what they are giving, it will help them to become sympathetic to other people's problems.

On the following Sunday, in Sunday groups and also in the main church services, the prayers may include a remembrance of the church visited, its clergy and people, and any cause which it may be concerned with or be supporting.

It would also be a kind gesture to invite the host church back to your own church on another occasion and to provide similar facilities for them. This will also encourage co-operation between churches.

Visiting cathedrals

Any cathedral within reach is always worth a visit. Cathedrals as well as churches are living witnesses of the continuity of the worship of God. In cathedrals not a single day goes by without public worship being offered to God, often two or three times. This has gone on for hundreds of years.

Some cathedrals have printed guide-books for children, which will show them round the building and tell them what to look for. They are usually reasonable in price, and if you are taking a party of children, it would be well to let the cathedral know beforehand how many books you are likely to want, so as to ensure that they have enough in stock for you. You may also wish to arrange for a verger or some other suitable person to act as guide to your party.

If whole families join in these church/cathedral visits (an involvement much to be encouraged), it would be wise to see if there is a nearby open space or similar facility where very young children can be left to play under adult supervision. If you are picnicking, check that there is a suitable place for it, with toilet facilities not too far away.

Some joint events which may be carried out with other churches

It is useful if several churches can get together to hold events such as children's festivals, etc. In the Anglican Church it may well be all the churches in a deanery; in the Methodist Church it may be the churches in a circuit; or it may simply be any group of churches in a given area. Such joint events can involve children, leaders and parents. For example, a group of leaders and others can meet to share an afternoon or whole day together for:

a) A service in one of the churches

Each group could bring its own banner, and the event could be followed by sports and a picnic tea. The theme of the service might be 'God's Family', for instance, and could include a procession, with a clergyman, a children's leader, and a church family (children and parents) from each of the participating churches taking part. Others present might also take part in the service by reading, leading prayers, etc.

One rural deanery visited a church in a neighbouring deanery and took their banners with them. At the end of the tour, they were due to walk to the local park, about a quarter of a mile away, for their picnic. It was a busy Saturday afternoon, and market-day, and the local guide was somewhat taken aback when the children lined up outside the church with their banners aloft. 'Are you bringing all those?' asked the guide, thinking of the thronged narrow streets, protruding sun-blinds, hanging baskets and so forth. 'Of course,' replied a teenage girl with a huge banner, 'We're Christians aren't we? Why shouldn't we show people?'

b) A drama/music festival

Each junior church group would produce an item. If the theme were, say, 'A festival of Saints', each children's group might do a short play or mime or song about a particular saint. Or the theme might be 'The church building' and could be centred on the hymn, 'We love the place, O God.'[13] Each children's group or several groups together might then interpret a different verse. Young children might take part in a similar activity based on the verses of 'All things bright and beautiful.'[14] Another theme might be 'The Bible', with interpretations of various books or characters.

c) An inter-church quiz

Teams from various churches in the area could participate.

d) A celebration of talents which God has given us

This could be arranged either as acted/sung items or as exhibition items, or both, with various children's groups interpreting different talents. These might range from common ones, such as uses of hands, eyes, ears, etc, to more unusual ones involving music, arts and crafts demonstrated by various children.

e) A joint inter-church exhibition

Similar to the local one, described on page 146 but with several churches taking part. This is very useful in giving ideas to other leaders, and also in giving parents and other adults an opportunity to see the wider work of the church with its children.

These are only a few ideas for occasions when leaders, parents and others can come together to learn about the church's work with children, and to get to know one another socially.

A Miscellany of further ideas mainly for meetings of clergy and leaders of children from single churches or from several churches of either the same or different denominations

Leaders receive great benefit from meeting together; they can exchange ideas, share problems, and find a deeper sense of understanding and commitment as fellow-Christians in the area. A few suggestions for such meetings are:

a) *Meetings to hear talks* on useful subjects such as:

* How to make visual aids
* Dance, drama and mime in the church and in its worship
* Under-privileged children, and how the church can help them
* Problem children — coping with their behaviour and understanding it
* New books, resources and teaching materials on the market

b) *Workshops* for pooling ideas, making visual aids, collages, models and wall charts, and generally 'messing about with paint, paper and glue'.

c) *A quiet afternoon or evening* for leaders to renew their strength in God; or a summer evening meeting in church, for a service of Holy Communion or Evensong. Either of these suggestions might be followed by refreshments and a general social gathering.

d) *A leaders' coffee evening or morning*, when leaders from several Sunday groups/churches can meet over coffee, preferably with the RE Adviser or other expert present, to share problems and ideas.

e) *An 'Any Questions' panel* for leaders in the area (and any others interested in the Christian upbringing of children), when experts in the field can come and answer questions, and initiate discussion from the audience. This type of thing can be very valuable, even though there may not be a large number of people present. It gives leaders a chance to share their problems and ask advice of others in an informal way.

All-age social activities

The church, as God's family, should not only pray and learn together; if we are going to get to know one another and really become a family, then we must also play together. Some people interpret this in the rather overworked word 'fellowship'. Nevertheless, it is a very good way to become friends with our fellow-Christians.

A certain church, like many others, had a fairly well-organised party planning system which took place every year around Christmastime. The Sunday school (as it then was) had a party of fun, games, sticky buns, ice-cream and crisps, etc for all the children; the youth club had a rather more grown-up affair; the Mothers' Union had their party; the bell-ringers had theirs, and so did most of the other church organisations. All this was great fun and everyone seemed to enjoy it, as separate organisations. But it did nothing for the church *as a family*. So it came to be suggested that there should be one big party instead of seven or eight separate smaller ones.

The local secondary school hall was hired, as it was the only place capable of holding the 200+ people who were expected to come.

The whole congregation was invited to this Grand Church Party — and they came, from toddlers to grannies. It started in mid-afternoon one Saturday after Christmas (when most of the other private parties people were involved in were out of the way).

The first item was games for the children, with some

stalwart adults joining in. Those who did not feel active enough to join in sat around and laughed at the fun, or maybe occasionally acted as a goalpost or something equally unenergetic. These games were organised and run, *not* by the Sunday group leaders but by other adults from the congregation. (It is amazing what hidden talents there are available once one starts looking for them!) The reason that the Sunday group leaders were barred was because the children knew them too well, and if the leaders had run the games, the children might have felt that it was just another Sunday-school-type party with a few extra grown-ups around. The idea was for them to realise that they were all part of the family of God, though obviously they would only assimilate this idea sub-consciously. Thus the children got to know other adults in the church, while the Sunday group leaders remained discreetly in the background.

At about 4.30 pm, the babies and toddlers had their party tea and were then taken home to bed. Older children (6 or 7+) stayed and joined the main tea (for adults and older children), at about 6 pm. This was a buffet affair and consisted of something contributed by everyone (a few sandwiches, a cake, a few biscuits, etc), so that the cost of the party was merely limited to the hire of the hall and some other sundries. This kept the cost of the tickets at a very modest price.

After tea there were more games, in which both children and adults joined, or watched if they preferred, together with various bits of homespun entertainment provided by members of the church.

The net result was that a number of Christians got to know a number of other Christians, and the family of God became more firmly cemented in that town. Henceforth it was felt that the Grand Church Party should be an annual affair.

The same sort of idea might apply to other social activities in which a church can be involved, and those planning the activity should aim to include children every time. Why not a joint outing in the summer, for instance? Or a church family walk, or a picnic? All such events will help children, if included as they should be, to feel that they really belong and are welcome in the church family. Such occasions will be saying to them, 'You're one of us!'

Churches where children are increasingly involved in the worship and life of the whole church family tend to keep their children; whereas those who separate the children off and leave them entirely to a small band of Sunday school teachers/leaders continue to lose them. If we want the children to stay and grow up in the church, then we must really work at it. There is something wrong with a church which has no children or young people in it.

If we belong to God's family, then each child is part of 'our' family, and not just the responsibility of parents and leaders. They are a vulnerable part, however, so we must all do all we can to care for their spiritual lives. Once they feel they belong, they will be prepared to give us their complete trust, and we must not let them down.

We must create opportunities for the whole of God's family to be together and to experience what it means to be part of a Christian community, learning, working, worshipping and playing together. It is all part of the responsibility of every single person who professes and calls himself Christian; he must love God and his fellow-men — even the youngest of them. The mission field starts on one's own doorstep among one's own neighbours.

Conclusion

The ideas in this book are but part of the church's contribution to the healthy growth and spiritual development of the young. Good spiritual foundations can seldom be laid or fostered without the co-operation of parents and the support of other members of the worshipping community. The task cannot be left to the Sunday group leaders and clergy alone. We must *all* help to give children a sense of belonging to Christ; only then will they have the roots to enable them to grow and to live by Christian values, thus leading to happier lives.

To every Christian adult the message comes in the words of Christ himself: 'Whoever receives one such child in my name receives me; and whoever receives me, receives not me but him who sent me' (Mk 9:37). 'Let the children come to me, do not hinder them; for to such belongs the kingdom of God' (Mk 10:14).

Notes

1 Although the words 'Sunday school', 'teacher' and
'class' are still in use in many churches today, it is felt
that they are perhaps not the best words to use. They
are too reminiscent of school, which is apt to give the
children the unconscious thought that because it is
'school', it is a place which one leaves for ever when
one is sixteen or so. This may contribute to the fact
that many children leave the church during their
teenage years, probably regarding confirmation as a
sort of 'church leaving certificate'. The words 'leader'
and 'group' would at least help the child to realise
that he is not in a class with a teacher and that church
is something different.

Some parishes refer to their children's sessions as
'Junior Church', which is certainly an improvement
as it connects the idea with the church in the child's
mind; and 'church' is a place for grown-ups as well as
children.

When Robert Raikes and his contemporaries
began Sunday schools some 200 years ago, they were
schools in the more general sense of the word, because the children, who often had little or no education, had to be taught to read and write.

2 Alfred, Lord Tennyson, 'The Passing of Arthur', line
415.

3 C Wesley, 'Gentle Jesus, meek and mild', *Hymns Ancient & Modern Revised* (Hymns Ancient and Modern Ltd: Norwich, 1972), no 451.

4 Mrs C F Alexander, 'All things bright and beautiful', ibid, no 442.

5 Bishop Christopher Wordsworth, 'O Lord of heaven and earth and sea', ibid, no 480.

6 G Brattle, *Sing to God* (Scripture Union Publishing: London, 1971), no 41.

7 Archangels are chief angels.

8 Holy Communion, *The Alternative Service Book 1980* (Oxford University Press/A R Mowbray & Co Ltd), p 131.

9 General Synod Board of Education, *Children in the Way* (Church House Publishing, 1988), p 88, para 7.41.

10 Ibid, para 7.40.

11 Ibid, p 84–5, para 7.24–7.31.

12 Ibid, p 87, para 7.38.

13 W Bullock and Sir H W Baker, 'We love the place, O God', *Hymns Ancient & Modern Revised*, no 242.

14 Mrs C F Alexander, *op cit*.

What About The Children?

A practical handbook for those who work with children

by Sally Hudspeth

'I'm finding it hard to hold the attention of the children for more than ten minutes. I wonder where I can get some ideas.'

'You think you've got a problem. I don't know who's going to teach our children at church. We don't have any Sunday School teachers.'

'We do, but there's no one to lead the children in worship. They just do lessons all the time. Or play games.'

Any of these situations familiar to you? Sally Hudspeth has taught children for many years, both in school and church. Her experience gives her a wealth of practical wisdom denied to many, but in this book she shares that experience and gives clear guidelines for all those who have a group of children to face, whether there are 5 or 105 waiting to be entertained . . .

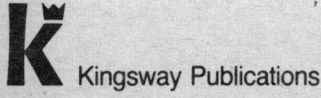

Kingsway Publications